THE WAR IN PICTURES

FOURTH YEAR

ODHAMS PRESS LIMITED
LONG ACRE, LONDON, W.C. 2

ALLIES CONTROL THE SEAS.
Despite the efforts of the U-boats, the navies of the United Nations keep the trade routes open.

THE TURNING OF THE TIDE

When the full story of the Second World War comes to be written the historians may well judge that the autumn of the year 1942 marked the turning-point in this mighty struggle for the freedom of all the nations. Japan's ruthless and unprovoked attack on Pearl Harbour in December, 1941, extended the war across the two hemispheres, but at the same time it brought the entire military and industrial power of the U.S.A. to the side of Great Britain and her Allies.

Grave setbacks and grievous losses were to be suffered by the United Nations before many months had passed; losses which, so far as the British Empire was concerned, were without parallel in history. Nevertheless, we may view 1942 as a year of bold planning and satisfactory, if not spectacular, achievement. For as it drew towards its close the Allies had definitely passed from the stage of defence and preparation to that of offensive action. While the greatest battles and the hardest fighting still lay ahead, the promise of victory could now be discerned more clearly. In 1943 the careful and secret planning by the leaders of the United Nations came, at last, to fruition, and by the end of the fourth year of war the first of the final victories over the Axis countries had been realized with the unconditional surrender of Italy.

In order that the reader may appreciate the special significance of the year of war to be reviewed in this volume, it is first necessary to recall some of the chief events of the previous twelve months.

Japan's lightning victories in the Far East came like a thunderbolt. They exceeded by far, in range and in speed, all the Nazi conquests in Europe two years earlier. In less than four months after Pearl Harbour the Japanese had completely overrun the Dutch East Indies, the greater part of the Philippines and the whole of British Malaya, and had seized control of some of the world's most precious raw materials. They had also captured two of the most important U.S. naval bases in the Pacific, namely, Guam and Wake Islands. The loss of Singapore on 15 February, 1942, was the greatest single military disaster which Britain had suffered since the fall of France two years earlier.

AUSTRALIAN SUCCESS IN NEW GUINEA. During the long campaign in Papua, New Guinea, the Australian troops played a part of conspicuous gallantry. Fighting for many months amid dense jungle and wild mountainous territory—to which terrible weather conditions added a further handicap—they drove the Japanese back to a narrow strip of land along the northern shores of the island and so relieved the enemy's threat to Australia. This picture shows Australian infantry advancing through a muddy jungle track to attack the Japanese at Milne Bay.

Without pause the Japanese continued their ambitious military plan to conquer and dominate the whole of the Far East and the Pacific, advancing into Burma and striking hard at Java, the last remaining foothold of the Allies in the Dutch East Indies. By cutting the Burma Road they dealt a severe blow at the heroic Chinese armies, who were now deprived of their last effective supply line. Nevertheless, in spite of this appalling handicap, China still kept on fighting and the morale of her people was as high as it had ever been. After the fall of Rangoon the enemy threatened the security of India and by their total occupation of the Dutch East Indies on 17 April directly menaced Allied sea communications between the Pacific and Indian Oceans.

Not until the Battle of the Coral Sea, fought on 4-8 May, 1942, was the furious tide of Japanese aggression slowed down and the immediate peril to Australia removed. This battle may be seen as one of the major naval engagements of the Second World War, and one which certainly turned the tide in the Far East. Another crippling blow at the enemy's naval power—on which the whole of Japanese strategy depended—was struck by the American Navy at the Battle of Midway Island on 3-7 June. This finally settled the balance of sea power in the Pacific in favour of the Allies. Pearl Harbour was at last avenged.

Meanwhile the Allied outlook in the Middle East and on the Russian front was not especially encouraging. Between November, 1941, and January, 1942, the Eighth Army, under General Auchinleck, had advanced into Libya to El Agheila. But owing to the difficulties of maintaining supplies through the Mediterranean it was impossible to hold much of the territory won, and the Eighth Army was forced to retire to Gazala. After a long pause, during which Rommel was able to reinforce his armies more rapidly than General Auchinleck, the Germans launched a powerful offensive on 26 May, 1942. A few weeks later Tobruk had fallen and the Eighth Army was retiring to El Alamein inside Egypt. By 1 July Rommel was only sixty miles west of Alexandria and the Suez Canal lay almost within his reach.

Greatest German drive in Russia

While the Afrika Korps was advancing in the Western Desert the German Armies in Russia, now recovering from their rough handling by the Red Army in the previous winter, were preparing another great summer offensive. This they launched on 28 June in the sector north of Kharkov, throwing 2,000,000 men or more into the operations. The enemy's plan was, by advancing to the lower Volga, to cut off the Russian armies from their main oil supplies and to gain control of some of the chief Russian coalfields and arsenals. The parallel German thrusts towards the Volga and, later, in the Caucasus and towards the Suez Canal through Egypt, were actually closely synchronized parts of an ambitious Nazi dream to link up their forces in the Near East where the rich Caucasian oilfields, together with those of Irak and Iran, were such a tempting prize. The Germans clearly aimed at seizing full control of the Mediterranean, encircling neutral Turkey and thereby cutting the Allied southern supply route to Russia via the Persian Gulf. Had this scheme materialized the Allies might have faced disaster.

Simultaneously with their offensive and break-through south of Kursk, the enemy launched a powerful attack against Sevastopol on the Black Sea. Its fall on 1 July gave them a useful foothold from which to carry out landing operations south of the Caucasian Mountains. The strength of the Russian Black Sea Fleet, however, discouraged this. During July and August the German offensive along the Eastern Front gathered fury, and for many weeks both sides, suffering enormous casualties, were locked together in the bloodiest fighting of the war. The fiercest battles were waged in the Don sector, where the enemy succeeded in throwing huge mechanized and infantry forces across the river Don at Voronezh. Finding themselves halted here they had to switch their armies south by a different route for the coming assault on Stalingrad.

The Battle for Stalingrad, with which the fourth year of war opened, was a conclusive turning-point in the present world conflict on land and its repercussions were widespread. For three months the Red Army put up an unparalleled

RUSSIA FIGHTS ON THE SEA AS WELL AS ON LAND. Although the great continuous land offensives carried on by the Red Army naturally took the predominant place in the news from Russia during the fourth year of war, much good work—both offence and defence—was done on the seas round her coasts. For instance, units of the Russian Navy, operating in the Black Sea, aided the Red Army's spectacular advance in the Caucasus by foiling the enemy's plans for the large-scale landing of troops along the southern coast. This picture shows a line of the latest Russian torpedo boats setting out on a fighting assignment from their base at a Black Sea port.

defence of this bastion of the Volga. Here the Germans encountered the most bitter opposition since their first attack on the Soviet Union; here, instead of advancing hundreds of miles in a matter of weeks, they advanced merely by yards and feet in a similar period. The savage hand-to-hand fighting, not only in the city's battle-scarred streets and bomb-blasted squares but even on the various floors of buildings, gave to this death struggle a nightmarish, almost unreal, quality. Never before had the defenders of a city displayed such irrepressible courage and dogged tenacity. Never had an enemy to pay such a high price for a conquest that was to prove in vain.

Despite his vast losses in both men and war material the German commander, von Bock, continued to throw in fresh reserves which were, nevertheless, mown down and annihilated by the Russian defenders. But by the middle of November it was plain that the struggle for Stalingrad, which hitherto had seemed to promise a certain German victory or, at best, a stalemate, had turned in favour of the defenders. The offensives launched by the Red Army north and south of the city on 19 November succeeded in smashing through the enemy's main lines and the terrible three-months siege was relieved. The ultimate triumph of the Red Army at Stalingrad was the encirclement and annihilation of the German Sixth Army and the capture of its commander, von Paulus.

The victory at Stalingrad heralded the spectacular winter offensive by the Red Army which, by the last days of 1942, was driving westwards towards the Donetz basin and Rostov and was also threatening the ill-equipped German forces in the snow-covered Caucasus. The enemy's sweeping gains in the Caucasus, which in November had put the Grozny oilfields in immediate danger, achieved nothing. Here, as on the Don front, the German armies were rolled back with ever greater speed than that at which they had previously advanced. Before the end of February, 1943, every Nazi had been cleared from the Caucasus.

BATTLE OF EL ALAMEIN

While the fighting for Stalingrad was reaching its climax, the Eighth Army began its westward advance from Egypt as the first stage of the task of clearing the Axis forces out of Africa. On 23 October General Montgomery launched an attack on El Alamein which, by its initial success, drove the enemy finally from the gates of Egypt and robbed him of his last hope of gaining the prizes which lay beyond its frontiers. The Battles of El Alamein and Stalingrad together foiled the enemy's grandiose scheme to which reference has already been made; namely, the linking of his main armies in the Near East and the seizure of the rich oilfields of the Caucasus and Irak and Iran.

The Eighth Army's break-through at El Alamein and General Montgomery's brilliant outflanking movement there completely shattered the Axis defences. More than 40,000 prisoners were taken in the first few days and the beaten enemy was soon in full retreat along the coast road, subjected to almost continuous "strafing" by the Western Desert Air Force. Such was the speed of the Eighth Army's pursuit, despite enemy minefields and demolitions, that by 9 November British troops had crossed the frontier into Libya. Benghazi was reached and occupied on 20 November. Still the battered Afrika Korps was chased westwards, constantly harassed by the R.A.F., until on 23 January, exactly three months after the offensive at El Alamein began, the Eighth Army occupied Tripoli, the last remaining town of the former Italian Empire in Africa.

LANDINGS IN NORTH AFRICA

The real beginning of major developments in the Mediterranean, however, was the British and American landings in French North Africa on 8 November. This was the greatest amphibious military operation in history, and the secrecy with which it was carried out assured its success. The object of these landings was to hasten the clearance of the Axis armies from African soil and to prepare the way for attack on the southern part of the European mainland.

Soon after the Allies had occupied Oran and Algiers all Vichy resistance in French African territory collapsed, and the British and American Forces crossed into Tunisia. The Tunisian campaign was one of the most difficult of the war. From the start the Allies found themselves at a disadvantage through the inability to organize air power owing to lack of suitable airfields. The Germans had poured large forces by air into the north-east corner of the country immediately following the Allied landings and, consequently, had gained control of the best airfields around Tunis and Bizerta. They drew up a powerful line of defence in front of the main road and railway linking the two towns. Before the Allies could bring sufficient strength to bear on these Axis positions the enemy was able to assemble considerable

JAPANESE LOSE DUTCH OIL. During the time when the Japanese were rapidly extending their lightning conquests in the Far East, the Allies adopted the policy of "scorched earth" wherever and whenever it was possible to do so. When the Dutch were compelled to retreat from the Tandjong area of Java in the spring of 1942 they set fire to the huge oil storage tanks there. They also destroyed a vast amount of machinery and thousands of transport vehicles which would have been of much value to the enemy. The picture shows the oil tanks burning.

R.A.F. "BOSTONS" ATTACK FRENCH STEEL WORKS. During the spring and summer of 1943 the British and American air forces steadily increased their daylight attacks on industrial targets in Germany and enemy-occupied territory. Factories and communication centres which the Nazis had once thought to be relatively immune from the attention of Allied bombers now received more frequent and more devastating blows. Pictured

above is a heavy and concentrated raid on the important steel and armament works at Denain, France, carried out by a strong force of "Bostons." The factories were attacked from heights ranging from barely fifty feet to above 1,500 feet, and although the industrial objectives suffered severely, damage to residential property in the neighbourhood was remarkably light. The picture shows a "Boston" (bottom, centre) at almost roof-top height.

EIGHTH ARMY DRIVES THE AXIS WESTWARDS. Many daring and highly successful actions were fought by British and Dominion troops as they continued their advance through the Libyan Desert from El Alamein in pursuit of the much-harassed German and Italian armies. This dramatic action picture was taken during General Montgomery's great outflanking movement on the road towards Matratin between El Agheila and Sirte. It shows British advanced infantry with bayonets and rifles charging through a smoke screen to storm an enemy position.

reinforcements from Sicily and Italy. This was the prime reason for the delay in the whole campaign; the initial advantage was unavoidably lost by the Allies.

From the German point of view the Tunisian campaign could have been nothing more than an attempt to stage a large-scale delaying action. The German High Command were trying to hold the Tunisian bridgehead for as long as possible so as to prepare the defence of Sicily and Southern Italy, which, once the Allies had gained Tunis and Bizerta, would become the objective of attack from the other side of the Mediterranean. But a decisive stage was reached directly the Eighth Army broke through the Mareth Line, where General Montgomery repeated the same successful outflanking movement as at El Alamein. The subsequent advance by the Eighth Army northwards through Sfax and the link-up with the British First Army and the Americans from the west, sealed the fate of the Axis in Tunisia. With the occupation of Tunis and Bizerta the retreating enemy was trapped in the narrow Cape Bon peninsula with his back to the sea and little chance of escape. All resistance ended on 13 May; Africa was at last set free from Nazi and Fascist tyranny. Malta, whose people had so long and valiantly borne the Nazi air terror, was now relieved.

Meanwhile, in the far north of Russia the Red Army had scored another notable victory. On 18 January, following a fortnight's heavy fighting, the siege of Leningrad was raised after sixteen months. The Russians launched their two-pronged offensive on 12 January from the west bank of the Neva and from the area south of Lake Ladoga. Aided by the Red Fleet and coastal batteries, the land forces penetrated powerful German defences to a depth of nine miles, and on 18 January the siege was raised when the two Russian armies linked up. At least five German divisions were routed, and over 13,000 of the enemy killed. While the siege lasted the people of Leningrad suffered great privations. The only link between the beleaguered city and the rest of Russia had been by air and across the frozen ice of Lake Ladoga, over which food, fuel and munitions reached the four million inhabitants. Nevertheless, the normal life of Leningrad went on, and many of its important war factories continued production throughout the siege, although during the severe winter months hundreds of wooden houses had to be pulled down to provide much-needed fuel.

In the Far East the beginning of the fourth year of the war saw the Allies on the offensive against the Japanese in the Solomons and New Guinea and continuing the process of wearing down the enemy's shipping. Having completely recovered their own power at sea they were now able to set about the task of throwing the Japanese back, island by island. By September the Americans had regained full control of the main islands in the Solomons group after three weeks of heavy fighting. The combined sea and air power now at the Allies' command allowed the Americans and Australians to stabilize their foothold on the islands. Moreover, repeated attempts by the Japanese to recover Guadalcanal during the autumn of 1942 all ended in failure. During these sporadic landings the enemy lost at least fifty warships and transports against Allied losses of one aircraft carrier, seven cruisers and fifteen other vessels. Finally, on 9 February, Japanese G.H.Q. announced that their troops had evacuated Guadalcanal. This virtually ended the Solomons campaign which had cost the enemy more than 50,000 men, of whom 30,000 were killed or drowned in the great sea battle of mid-November.

By their landings on the north coast of Papua, New Guinea, in March, 1942, the Japanese took a further step towards the Australian mainland. They proceeded to advance through the jungles of the Owen Stanley Mountains in a thrust for Port Moresby, the chief Allied base on the southern coast, less than 400 miles from Port Darwin. In an attempt to avoid the mountains and take a short cut towards Port Moresby the enemy landed in force at Milne Bay, at the extreme west, on 27 August. This failed disastrously, for Allied troops and planes were in waiting there, and after suffering heavy casualties the bulk of the enemy forces was hastily withdrawn. Meanwhile, the Australians advanced northwards, and after bitter jungle fighting drove the invaders back to a narrow strip of the north coast. Buna was taken by Australian troops on 19 December and with the recapture of Buna Mission and the Sanananda area the whole of Papua was cleared of Japanese by mid-January after some of the toughest fighting ever known.

One of the most favourable aspects of the fourth year of the war was the steady improvement of the

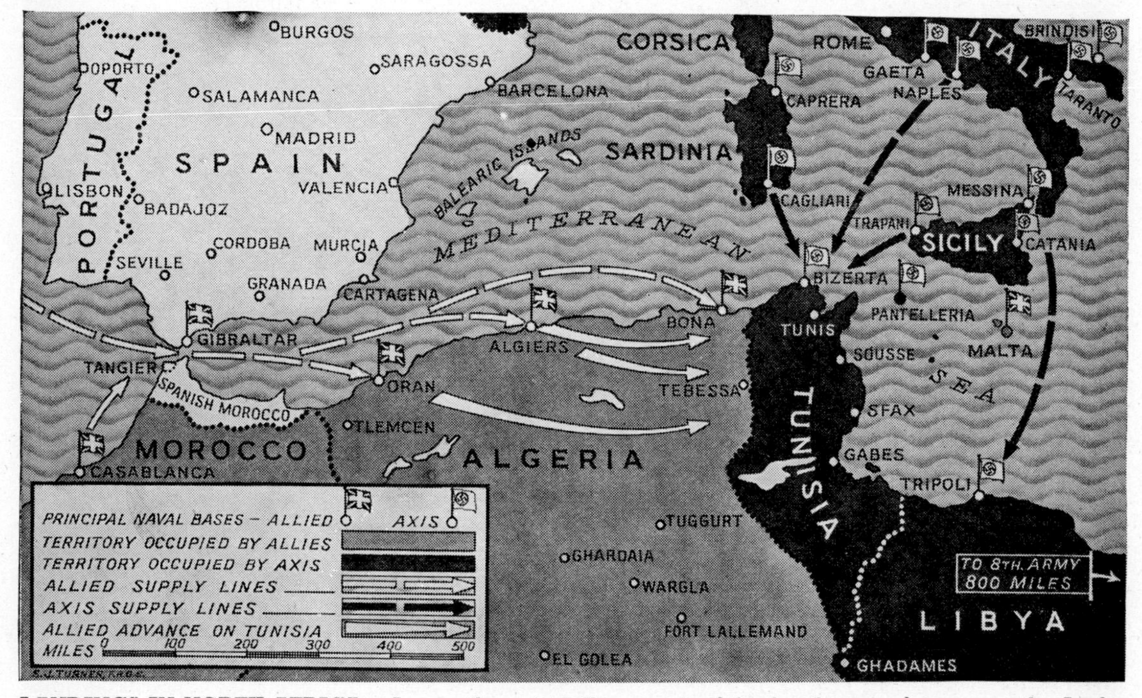

LANDINGS IN NORTH AFRICA. Among the outstanding events of the fourth year of war were the Anglo-American landings in French North Africa on 8 November, 1942. This map, specially drawn by S. J. Turner, F.R.G.S., shows the relative positions of the Allies and the Axis at that time. The arrows indicate the supply lines of both sides, and also the route taken by the vast Allied convoys through the Western Mediterranean.

RUSSIAN PRISONERS ON FORCED LABOUR. While the Germans pushed deeper into the Caucasus the problem of transport across the snow-covered mountains became increasingly difficult. In defiance of the international convention relating to prisoners of war, the Germans put captured Red Army men, under the threat of starvation, to the hard task of carrying munitions and supplies across frozen passes. The picture above shows hundreds of laden and half-starving Russian prisoners crossing the path over a glacier under Nazi guard.

Allied struggle against the U-boats. In the previous twelve months British losses had been grievously heavy owing to the U-boat "pack" methods in the busiest shipping areas of the Atlantic. The position had been aggravated because, with the Mediterranean closed, all supplies to the Middle East, India and Australia had to make the long voyage round the Cape. Here our shipping was exposed to the peril of the U-boats which were at that time concentrating their strength in the mid-Atlantic "Narrows" between the West African coast and Brazil (the ocean is only 1,600 miles wide here). When the port of Dakar and the whole of West Africa came under Allied control in November, 1942, the danger was considerably eased. Apart from being robbed of many secret bases they had used under Vichy connivance, the U-boats operating in the "Narrows" were now well within range of British and American shore-based aircraft. Brazil also, having previously declared war on the Axis, could now use its fleet and air force against the U-boats on the opposite side of the Atlantic gap.

BRITISH BOMBERS BLAST GERMAN WAR INDUSTRIES. The "Avro-Lancaster" four-engined bombers, pictured above, are units of the huge and ever-growing fleet of Allied warplanes which carried out the systematic destruction of the war industries of the Reich. The "Lancaster" has a maximum speed of more than 300 miles per hour, and carries a crew of seven. Its normal bomb load is approximately 15,000 pounds.

By the spring of 1943 the combined shipping losses of the United Nations were the lowest since the war began and, moreover, there was a far greater tonnage afloat. That the Germans were still waging their U-boat campaign in the Atlantic was clear, but now much more powerful means of defence as well as offence against them had been put into effect. The greater success against the U-boats was partly due to the increased use of long-range aircraft for attacking, as well as locating them. (In an eight-day battle at the beginning of May, ten U-boats out of a pack of twenty-five which made thirty attacks on an Atlantic convoy were destroyed by escort ships of the Royal Navy and aircraft of the Royal Canadian Air Force.) Another important factor was the heavy and sustained bombing of the enemy's chief U-boat bases, such as Hamburg and Lorient, and the industrial centres where U-boat parts were manufactured.

The early months of 1943 saw a considerable increase in the bombing of vital targets in Germany and enemy-occupied countries by home-based aircraft of the R.A.F. The air onslaught

SICILY INVADED

By landing in Sicily on 10 July, 1943, Allied troops regained a foothold in Europe for the first time since the collapse of France and the retreat from Dunkirk

PARATROOPS IN ACTION. The use of paratroops for aiding land operations has been developed by all the belligerents since war began. The Germans used them with success in Holland, France, Norway, Greece and elsewhere during the earlier stages of the war. Since then British and U.S. paratroops have been in action in many parts of the world. The picture shows British paratroops descending over Tunisia.

against Germany was now maintained for much longer periods both by day and night and British airmen flew deeper into the Reich than ever before and with heavier loads. In this new phase of the air war the R.A.F. adopted " saturation " tactics in raids on such important munitions centres as Cologne, Essen, Hamburg, Berlin and Mannheim. Night bombers from Britain also made numerous flights across the Alps to bomb industrial and railway centres in Northern Italy and Italian supply bases for the Axis armies in North Africa and Sicily. The weight and accuracy of this resolute bombing were certainly a decisive factor in bringing about the fall of Mussolini and the unconditional surrender of Italy.

The Russian summer offensive, which was preceded by many weeks of widespread operations against enemy bases and lines of communication by the Red Air Force, was launched on 15 July in the Orel sector, where the Red Army pierced strong German fortifications and advanced twenty-eight miles in three days. This immediately followed on the failure of a German attempt to break the Russian defences between Kursk and Orel; an attempt which cost the enemy nearly 3,000 in killed alone. Despite bad weather and the most bitter opposition, the Red Army achieved great success in their triple thrust towards Orel, and after three weeks of desperate fighting the city fell on 5 August. Orel, one of the most important German bastions in Russia, had been in enemy hands ever since October, 1941. On the same day the Red Army recaptured the town of Byelgorod. This great double victory finally gave the lie to the German legend that the Russians were unable to wage a summer offensive.

By the beginning of September the Red Army was advancing all along the front from the Smolensk sector southwards to the Donetz basin. While powerful Russian forces were driving from Orel towards Bryansk, a new offensive developed east of Kharkov. With the recapture of this city for the second time on 23 August the way lay open for the Red Army's sweeping advance into the Ukraine. So at the end of the fourth year of the war the German armies on the Eastern Front were staging one of the greatest retreats in military history, with the winter months still before them.

Meanwhile, important moves were being made by the United Nations in the Mediterranean area. After the final capitulation of the Axis armies in North Africa our Middle East Air Forces began heavy and widespread attacks both on the mainland of Italy and also on the strategic island bases around its shores. This "softening-up" operation on the enemy's defences, harbours, shipping, roads and railways was the prelude to the long-expected attack on the Nazis' self-styled "Fortress of Europe."

The Allied plan of campaign to achieve a solid foothold in Southern Europe was conceived as a series of leaps. The small island of Pantelleria surrendered to British troops on 11 June after being subjected to terrific day and night attacks from the air and bombardment from the sea. This island, situated roughly midway between Cape Bon in Tunisia and Malta, had long been the centre of Axis mine-laying operations in the Central Mediterranean. Its occupation was essential to afford the Allies complete control of the Sicilian "Narrows"—a prerequisite for the coming invasion of Sicily and Italy. It also gave them a useful jumping-off ground for larger amphibious operations nearly thirty miles closer to the southern coastline of Europe.

The occupation of Sicily, which was begun by British and U.S. troops with powerful airborne forces on 10 July, was another vital preliminary step in the larger plan. This island was by far the most strongly defended of the three that might have been selected (the others being Sardinia and Corsica) and its occupation was completed in a little less than six weeks. Sicily was chiefly important on account of its airfields. These totalled nearly fifty scattered about the island, and for many months they had been used to good purpose by the Germans. Now these airfields were urgently required by the Allies as advanced bases for the coming operations against the enemy on the Italian mainland. The attack on Sicily by the Allies was their first experience of staging a landing on territory fully occupied and strongly defended by the Axis. Consequently, it provided many important lessons in amphibious warfare which would be of the utmost value when the time arrived for the major attack on occupied Europe. Above all else, it demonstrated the tremendous importance of air power when used in conjunction with land and sea operations.

On 3 September, 1943, the fourth anniversary of the outbreak of the Second World War, the Eighth Army crossed the Straits of Messina and gained its first foothold upon the toe of Italy. Thus invasion hour struck in Hitler's Europe just when his beaten armies were being rolled back across the Russian plains, and the terrorized peoples of the Balkans, France, Denmark and the rest were seething in revolt against the common foe.

FIRE BOMBS FALL OVER BURMA. This remarkable picture, taken from one of the attacking aircraft, gives an unusual and close-up view of a heavy load of incendiary bombs falling towards a river-side village in the Taungdaung district of Burma during a raid on some important Japanese positions on 20 November, 1942. Fifty or more of these fire bombs can be seen hurtling down towards the earth and their targets.

THE BATTLE FOR STALINGRAD

24 AUGUST—27 NOVEMBER, 1942.

After throwing large infantry and tank forces across the Don on 22-23 August, the Germans massed in strength for the final assault against Stalingrad. The enemy's terrific blows on land and from the air pressed the Russians back relentlessly towards the Volga. Plainly, he was prepared to throw in everything in order to seize this large and important industrial centre—the key to the whole Russian defensive system. Von Bock's initial thrust for Stalingrad from the north-west, begun on 24 August, was supported by masses of tanks and heavy artillery and hundreds of dive bombers. For days and nights battles raged with unparalleled ferocity at the city's approaches and appalling casualties were suffered by both sides. In determined counter-attacks on 2-7 September the Red Army threw the invaders back, though not before the outer defence ring had been penetrated deeply at many points. By 12-13 September German tanks and artillery, as well as large infantry forces, had entered the suburbs and industrial areas of Stalingrad. Fierce hand-to-hand fighting raged among houses and factory buildings in the northern part of the city. At times a floor of a building would be held by one side while the other held the floor below. So stubborn was the Russian resistance that the enemy, despite greatly superior numbers, advanced only by the yard and at bitter cost. Attack after attack was repulsed with heavy casualties to the Germans, and by 12 October all their infantry and tank thrusts had been temporarily halted. Meanwhile, Stalingrad was subjected to the heaviest mass air attacks of the war. Three-quarters of the city was smashed by the Luftwaffe. Defences were breached, buildings razed, civilians murdered in thousands; smoke and dust enveloped the whole of Stalingrad in a permanent cloud. Yet the spirit of the defenders was unbroken. Fierce German attempts to break through to the Volga were launched again in late October and, after regrouping his forces a second time, von Bock made his final bid to win Stalingrad on 12 November. It failed. The tide had turned, and on 19 November the Red Army started its offensive north and south of the city. A week later both forces joined up. Stalingrad was relieved after the terrible three-months' siege. Seventy thousand prisoners and vast booty fell to the Russian troops. This picture shows women crossing a devastated square on their way out of Stalingrad after the evacuation of women and children had been ordered.

STALINGRAD BEFORE THE SIEGE
Central Square, Stalingrad, with the Obelisk of Freedom, before the Hun invaders arrived.

BITTER DEFENCE OF STALINGRAD CONTINUES. In their desperate and unavailing attempts to capture the city, the Germans were thwarted time and again by the demolition tactics employed by the Russians, who did not hesitate to destroy storehouses, war factories, and armament works rather than allow their possession to the enemy. The history of warfare shows no more stubborn defence than that of Stalingrad. The pictures show: above, German transport approaching the Stalingrad battle area; top, right, enemy armoured units and artillery advance into the shambles of a suburb; bottom, right, Nazi soldiers find a former Russian factory a mass of ruins.

STALINGRAD WOMEN ENDURE WORST AERIAL BOMBARDMENT. The weeks of heavy air raids on Stalingrad, which preceded the street fighting, were the most severe experienced by any civil population up to that time. Yet while buildings were falling overhead, women in cellars and caves far below the streets were busily occupied on vital work. Here they filled shells and hand grenades for the Red Army soldiers who were feverishly stemming the enemy's advance. Only between the bombings were they able to crawl up into the open in order to get food and water and wood for fuel. Above ground, the nurses of the city carried on calmly, going from one Red Army defence post to another. The pictures show: left, Nazi soldiers watching a Stalingrad woman emerge from a cellar; top, right, women searching for belongings after an air raid; bottom, right, women come up after the bombing.

Stalingrad—the women who

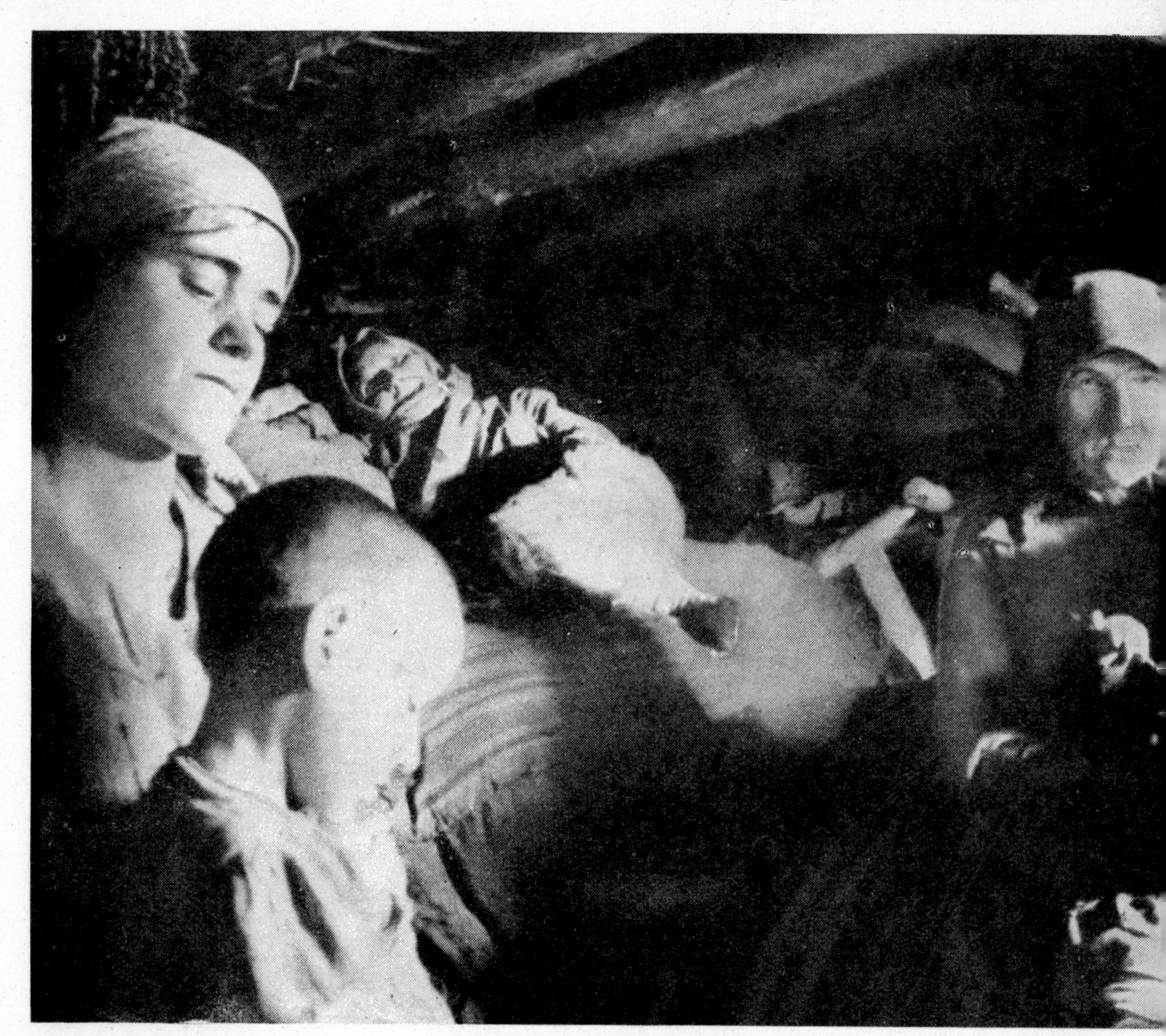

EPIC OF HUMAN SUFFERING. All women except nurses and doctors were ordered to leave Stalingrad, but many refused to go. These women and children, sheltering in a dug-out, make one of the most remarkable pictures of the war. Their set faces are instinct with quiet acceptance of their hazards. They seem to express the fierceness, the determination, the steel-like bravery, of the menfolk who battled above their heads day after day in a savage and bloody conflict that did not cease for three long months. The head-dress of the woman in the centre takes on the look of a helmet. In the shadows her cloak of cloth has the likeness of a proud soldier's armour, and unfaltering faith in victory arms her steady eyes. The baby on her knee, the child standing erect at her side, are equally unafraid. Their rough and crowded refuge shook to the constant thunder of guns, bombs and mines in the City of Storm above them. In that smashed city, sprawling along the Volga for thirty miles, scarcely a house still possessed a roof. Long ago (as far back as October, 1941) the vainglorious enemy trumpets had blared for victory, and Hitler had made his braggart proclamation to the German people, "Russia the enemy is broken, and will never rise again." In the same month of the same year Press Chief Otto Dietrich echoed his master, and again he trumpets of victory brayed—"I can tell you now—and I have the Fuehrer's authority for it—that for all military purposes Soviet Russia is done for as a result of the gigantic battles which have just been concluded." So much for 1941: so much for Germany's will-of-the-wisp victories, and for the lying trumpets of the Hun. Russia had risen at the command of the unshaken will of her people, and there was one gigantic battle not concluded—the epic battle for Stalingrad. Once again, at the beginning of the three months' battle for the city on the Volga, Hitler foolishly dared another prophecy. "Stalingrad will fall," he promised,

"you can be sure of it." Yet again Hitler was proved to lie, by the valour of the soldiers of the Red Army. The fires of hate and faith and anger quickened in the hearts of the people of Stalingrad, and transformed them all into avengers, tireless and invincible. They had one thought, one aim, one spirit, and one urgent cry—"Death to the invader!" In the streets of the ruined city, among the shells of houses, every heap of rubble was a stronghold, every ruin a fortress, every wrecked staircase a battlefield. Day by day, the mighty scale of the battle mounted in its terror. Thirteen thousand machine guns were at work on both sides; the Luftwaffe hammered the city incessantly, making 2,000 flights a day; in a single assault against the Red Barricade factory settlement the Germans employed hundreds of tanks and two divisions of infantry. For three months, along the roads to the city, Hitler flung vast numbers of troops, machines, guns and reserves into the monstrous weight of his offensive, while Stalingrad's defenders had only one way to get reinforcements of men and material—across the Volga. They controlled no roads. All they had was the perilous crossing of the river, through smoke, bombs, shells and machine gun fire. "Every one must be a stone of the city," General Chuykov, commanding the 62nd Soviet Army, told his men. "The city grows tired, the houses grow tired. We do not tire." The defenders of Stalingrad kept their proud pledge that no one ever retreated. In one bitter engagement Red Army men fought German tanks till there was nothing left for them to fight with. A Red Army soldier, clutching an anti-tank mine tightly in front of him, threw himself under an enemy tank, crying: "You won't get through." The tank blew up. Thus the soldiers of Stalingrad stubbornly died, but they did not tire. They did not retreat. They kept the Volga from the enemy, and after three months of desperate battle they drove him from Stalingrad.

FACTORY WORKERS SHOOT AT RAIDERS. As the fighting for Stalingrad reached a terrific climax, the defenders turned every house into a fortified point and every factory into a fortress. When the Germans began their massed air attacks early in September, workers throughout the city formed themselves into auxiliary anti-aircraft units. On 4 September forty-nine enemy bombers out of a force of 150 were shot down during a single raid on Stalingrad. The picture above shows members of a workers' battalion firing at German planes overhead.

RED ARMY COUNTER-ATTACKS NEAR STALINGRAD. On 4 September the Red Army launched a surprise counter-attack to the south-west of Stalingrad where the enemy had driven deeply into the city's main defences. In close-range fighting which lasted many hours, eleven German tanks were destroyed and 600 of the enemy killed. On the same day, to the north-west of the city, the Russians repulsed strong German tank attacks with heavy losses to the enemy. This dramatic picture shows Red Army infantry advancing with smoke-screen cover.

Ferocious air attacks or

BIGGEST ARCTIC CONVOY BATTLE. On 12 Sep ember began a violent battle between the largest Russia-bound convoy and a strong force o German aircraft and U-boats. Through four days and nights ceaseless attacks were made on the convoy by relays o d:ve bombers and submarines. Rear-Admiral Burnett, O.B.E., commanding the naval escort, described it as the worst torpedo-bombing attack of the war. But the enemy

paid dearly. Forty German planes were seen to crash into the sea and a large number were damaged, al for the loss of four British naval aircraft. Two U-boats were certainly sunk and four others hit. Although the ships in the convoy suffered losses (none to escorting warships) the great majority reached their destination. This picture, painted by Norman Wilkinson, P.R.I., shows the convoy being attacked by a swarm of enemy aircraft.

GERMANS FACE ANOTHER RUSSIAN WINTER

On 13 September the first w nter snows fell in the Caucasian Mountains. Here the Germans checked in their drive towards Grozny, had a foretaste of the conditions they would have to endure for months, and for these, despite Hitler's boasting, they were ill-prepared. On 14 September the enemy made slight gains south of the Terek River, but at heavy cost. Before the Red Army troops retired to new positions twenty-six snipers attached to one unit accounted for more than 1,000 Germans. In the next few weeks the enemy increased the fury of his attack against Stalingrad and, much farther south, in the Caucasus, drove on towards Tuapse, on the Black Sea. But the German High Command was complaining all the time of the increasing difficulties forced on their armies in Russia by bad weather. Most of their operations were reduced to solving transport problems, for in many places they relied on horse-drawn vehicles. Even lorries failed to negotiate roads which the snow and torrential rains so rapidly turned into seas of mud. The Russians, however, were much more mobile and were far better trained and equipped for winter fighting. The pictures show: right, a Red Army ski patrol on night reconnaissance; bottom, left, German lorries bogged in mud; and bottom, right, Red Army men clearing a snow-covered pass before the advance of their main forces.

SINKING OF THE "WASP." On 15 September the 14,700-ton U.S. aircraft-carrier "Wasp" was attacked and sunk by a Japanese submarine in the Coral Sea, although its loss was not announced officially until 26 October. At the time the ship was escorting a large supply convoy bound for Guadalcanal in the Solomon Islands which, however, reached port safely. Soon after the aircraft-carrier had been hit by three of the enemy torpedoes, she went down in an inferno of flame and smoke. Ninety per cent of the ship's crew managed to get away in time, and

were later picked up by escort vessels of the U.S. Navy. This remarkable picture, taken from the deck of one oi the ships in the convoy, shows dense clouds of smoke billowing from the abandoned aircraft-carrier just before she went down. The "Wasp," which was launched in 1939, had a proud record of war service. She earned much renown earlier in the year for her ferrying of reinforcements to Malta, making many voyages through the hazardous part of the Mediterranean. This aid was of vital importance in the defence of Malta.

Nazis round up wome

BRAVE YUGOSLAV PATRIOTS DEFY THE INVADER

Ever since the German and Italian armies marched into Yugoslavia on 6 April, 1941, the brave bands of native guerrillas in the mountains, forests and elsewhere continued their determined resistance against the hated invaders. In spite of repeated threats of shooting or torture in Nazi concentration camps the patriots never for a single day ceased their activities of sabotage and train-wrecking as well as open armed combat. In the latter part of the summer of 1942 the whole railway system of Yugoslavia was brought to a complete standstill for about ten days because of the widespread destruction done to tracks and rolling stock by the guerrillas. This brought about some considerable delay in the passage of German munitions and supplies which were being rushed through the Balkans to Rommel's harassed armies on the North African front. Many towns and villages throughout Yugoslavia were bombed from the air or burnt to the ground by gangs of infuriated young Nazis, but the remarkable resistance of the patriot forces continued seriously to upset the enemy's plans. This resistance much increased when the guerrillas were properly organized into groups under various brave guerrilla leaders. In September, about 20,000 German and Croat Fascist troops began an offensive against the guerrillas in a rugged part of the Bosnian mountains, near the little town of Banjalucka. After fifteen days of fierce fighting the enemy were beaten back at all points, leaving the patriot forces in control of the whole area. In a surprise counter-offensive, detachments of the Yugoslav Army attacked enemy garrisons, took 200 prisoners and wiped out several Croat detachments who were forcibly taking grain and crops from the peasants. The picture shows the Nazis rounding up innocent women and children in a village of the Bosnian hills. These were but a few of the hundreds o. peasants carried away to concentration camps as a reprisal for patriot defiance.

ANTI-AIRCRAFT FIRE FROM BRITISH SHIPS SCREENS A CONVOY TO MALTA.

ADVANCE IN NEW GUINEA. After the failure of .he Japanese landing at Milne Bay, Papua, on 27 August, the enemy made an unsuccessful thrust for Port Moresby on 10 September. The Australians began their advance into the Owen Stanley Mountains on 28 September and recaptured Myola and Kagi without opposition on 4 October.

While our troops penetrated the Kokoda Gap on the Buna side before making contact with the enemy, their progress was hampered by the often impassable jungle and torrential rains. The maintenance of supplies was a superhuman task for our troops under such conditions. Above, Australian and American soldiers making a road.

WAR IN THE JUNGLE. On the world's toughest battlefront, Australian and American Forces maintained progress in the New Guinea jungle throughout September and October. By 28 October the Australians had overcome determined Japanese resistance in the Alola area, just south of Kokoda. After five weeks fighting Kokoda was retaken on 2 November. Thus the enemy lost their last foothold on the Buna side of the Owen Stanley Mountains. The Australians proved superb jungle fighters in a country of almost trackless bush, where natives acted as carriers for ammunition and supplies. Natives are seen here crossing a jungle torrent by an improvised bridge.

BATTLE OF THE SOLOMONS. The reconquest of the Solomons by U.S. Marines, which began on 7 August, involved hard fighting. Fierce resistance was encountered on Guadalcanal, where the trapped Japanese Forces fought to the last man. On 3 September Marines attacked enemy landing-parties in the south-east of the group, and U.S. bombers scored hits on several ships. On 9-12 September strong Japanese air formations raided Tulagi and Guadalcanal, destroying twenty Allied planes. Despite these air attacks the Marines strengthened their positions on the main islands. Above, an American patrol carrying wounded back to a jungle base.

CROSSING NEW GUINEA JUNGLE

Behind the news of the Allied progress through the dense and almost trackless jungle of New Guinea lay the splendid work of Australian and U.S. engineers. They performed remarkable feats of road and bridge building under the most difficult conditions. These pictures show: top, left, Australian engineers building a suspension bridge over a wild jungle stream; top, right, bridging operations near Kokoda in the Owen Stanley range; below, American infantrymen wading through a swollen river.

END OF THE MADAGASCAR CAMPAIGN

On 8 November, 1942, all hostilities on the French island of Madagascar came to an end when an armistice, asked for by the French Governor-General, M. Annet, was signed between the British and Vichy military authorities. By the liquidation of the pro-Vichy administration a real threat to South Africa was removed. Moreover, the continuance of French sovereignty over the island was ensured. The final campaign in Madagascar opened early in September when the British Government announced that it was reluctantly obliged to undertake further military operations in the island. After the occupation of Diego Suarez in May, 1942, it was hoped that the Governor-General would allow the British to take whatever steps might be necessary to deny to the Axis bases and facilities elsewhere in the island. However, it became plain that he was unwilling to co-operate, and it was known that German agents in Madagascar had been helped by local officials on orders from Vichy. Operations to bring the whole of Madagascar under Allied control were begun on 10 September when British and Dominion troops, commanded by General Sir William Platt, made widespread landings on the west coast and also occupied Tamatave, the island's chief port, on the eastern side. By 20 September great advances had been made towards the interior of Madagascar, and British columns were steadily closing in on Antananarivo, the capital, which surrendered three days later. On 29 September all opposition in the northern part of the island had collapsed and operations were now confined to mopping up the remaining Vichy forces in the south. After four weeks of hard fighting, during which the Imperial troops made important gains, the last Vichy resistance began to collapse. During the whole campaign a total of more than 3,000 Europeans and Malagasy prisoners was taken and in the last few days over 1,000 Malagasy troops had deserted. In December, an agreement between the British Government and the French National Committee was signed in London which re-established French sovereignty over Madagascar and its dependencies. The picture shows native labourers clearing a road block during the advance.

SOUTH AFRICAN PREMIER VISITS BRITAIN. On 14 October Field-Marshal Smuts arrived in Britain by air for important consultations with the War Cabinet. On 21 October the famous Imperial statesman and soldier received a great welcome from the members of both Houses of Parliament whom he addressed at Westminster. In the course of a masterly speech he paid a warm tribute to the fortitude of the British people and the courage foresight and energy of its leader, Mr. Churchill. "The defence phase has now ended," he said. "The stage is set for the last, the offensive phase." In the picture above the Field-Marshal is seen delivering his address in the chamber. On the extreme left is the late Speaker of the House, Captain Fitzroy. To the right are Mr. Churchill and Viscount Simon. Mr. Lloyd George, the doyen of the House of Commons, presided over the meeting.

WOMEN GATHER THE HARVEST. In a broadcast speech on 11 October, Mr. R. S. Hudson, Minister of Agriculture, announced that the 1942 harvest in Britain had been the greatest on record. Britain started the war having lost 3,000,000 acres of agricultural land by building and several hundred thousand more for new aerodromes and factories. Nevertheless, the area under crops had increased by more than half since war began, and was, in fact, greater than in 1918. In the past summer thousands of women had played an important part on the land, tackling every kind of agricultural work. In this way men were released for other duties. The picture shows a Women's Land Army team cutting corn on a downland farm in the south of England. A few years ago this land was entirely derelict, but, as in many parts of the country, the demands of war transformed the scene.

FAMINE VICTIMS IN CHINA

During October, 1942, a famine occurred in the province of Northern Honan which threatened about 20,000,000 people with starvation. This was brought about by nearly two years of severe drought and a plague of locusts, unparalleled for centuries, which ruined the grain and rice fields. The blighted area extended over more than 20,000 square miles, and the districts which suffered most acutely were along the Yellow River in the neighbourhood of Cheng Chow, a town which lay only a dozen miles from the Japanese lines. While millions of people were able to leave the province for other parts of China, those who remained had to live on grass, straw, weeds and even the bark of trees. The disaster was greatly aggravated by Japanese troops who had for a long period been systematically burning fields, crops and villages in an attempt to put an end to the activities of the Chinese guerrilla bands. These gallant bands, in spite of many handicaps, had for long been a worry to the Japanese invaders. China was now in the sixth year of her war against Japan, and though she had lost much territory and had sacrificed countless lives her armies st'll stood firm in the path of the aggressor. The spirit of the country was still a glorious example for the world. So this additional disaster of famine was borne as bravely as were all her other sufferings. China's plight, however, was a serious one, especially as the loss of the Burma Road supp'y route made it extremely difficult for Britain, the U.S.A. and other Allies to come to her aid. The picture shows one of the many thousands of poor victims of what was probably the worst famine in the recorded history of China.

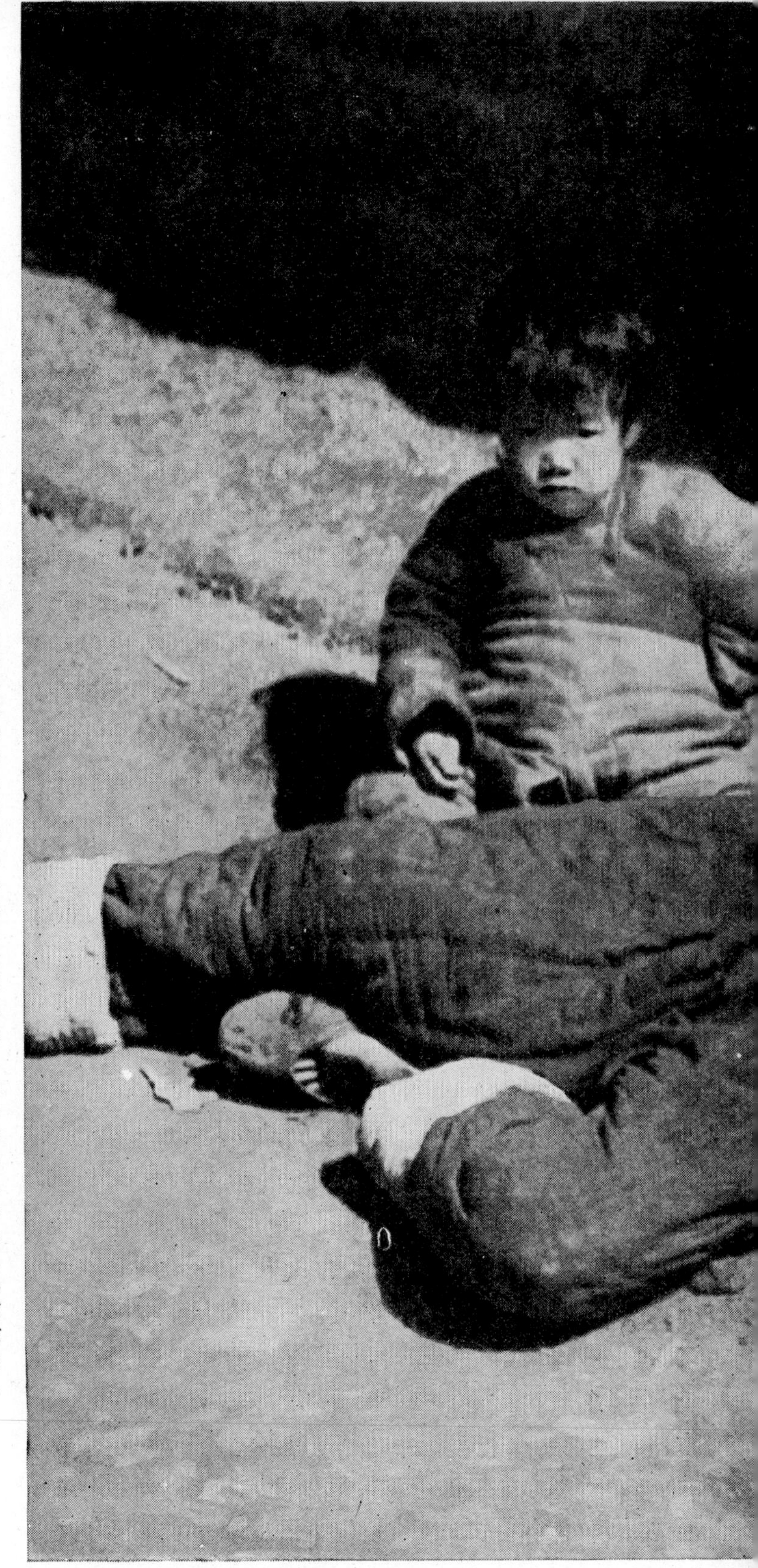

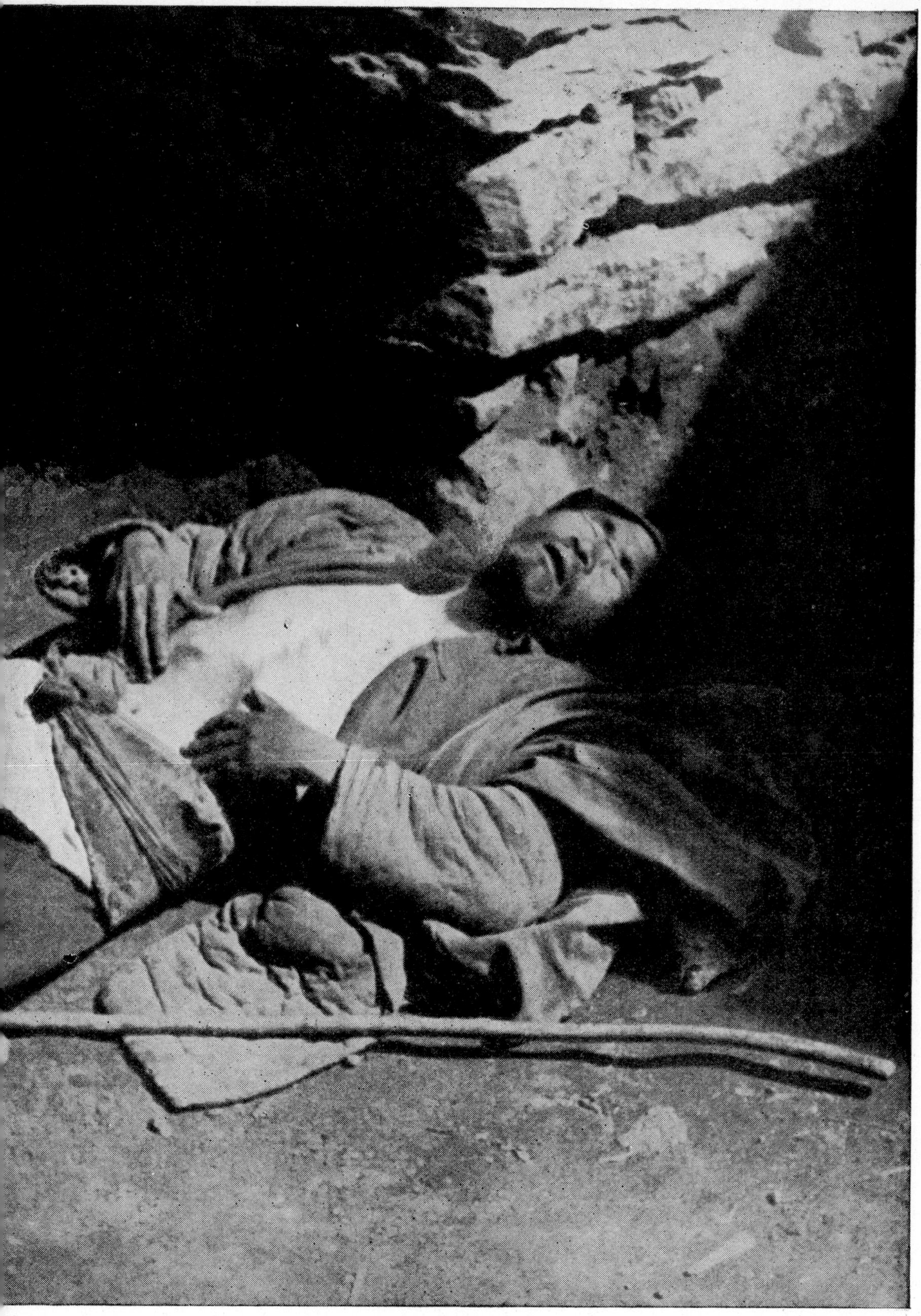

Carrying supplies to

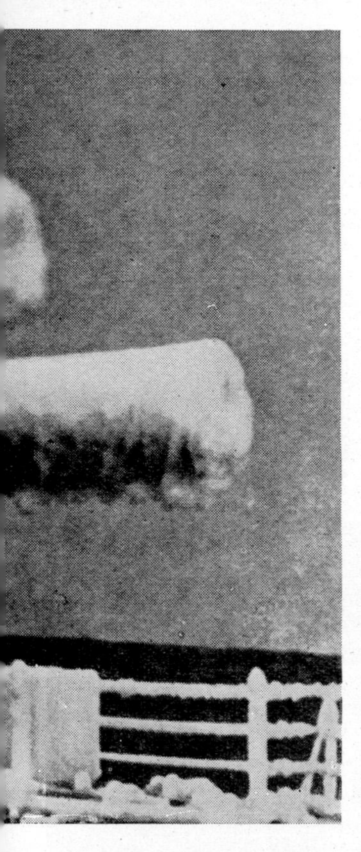

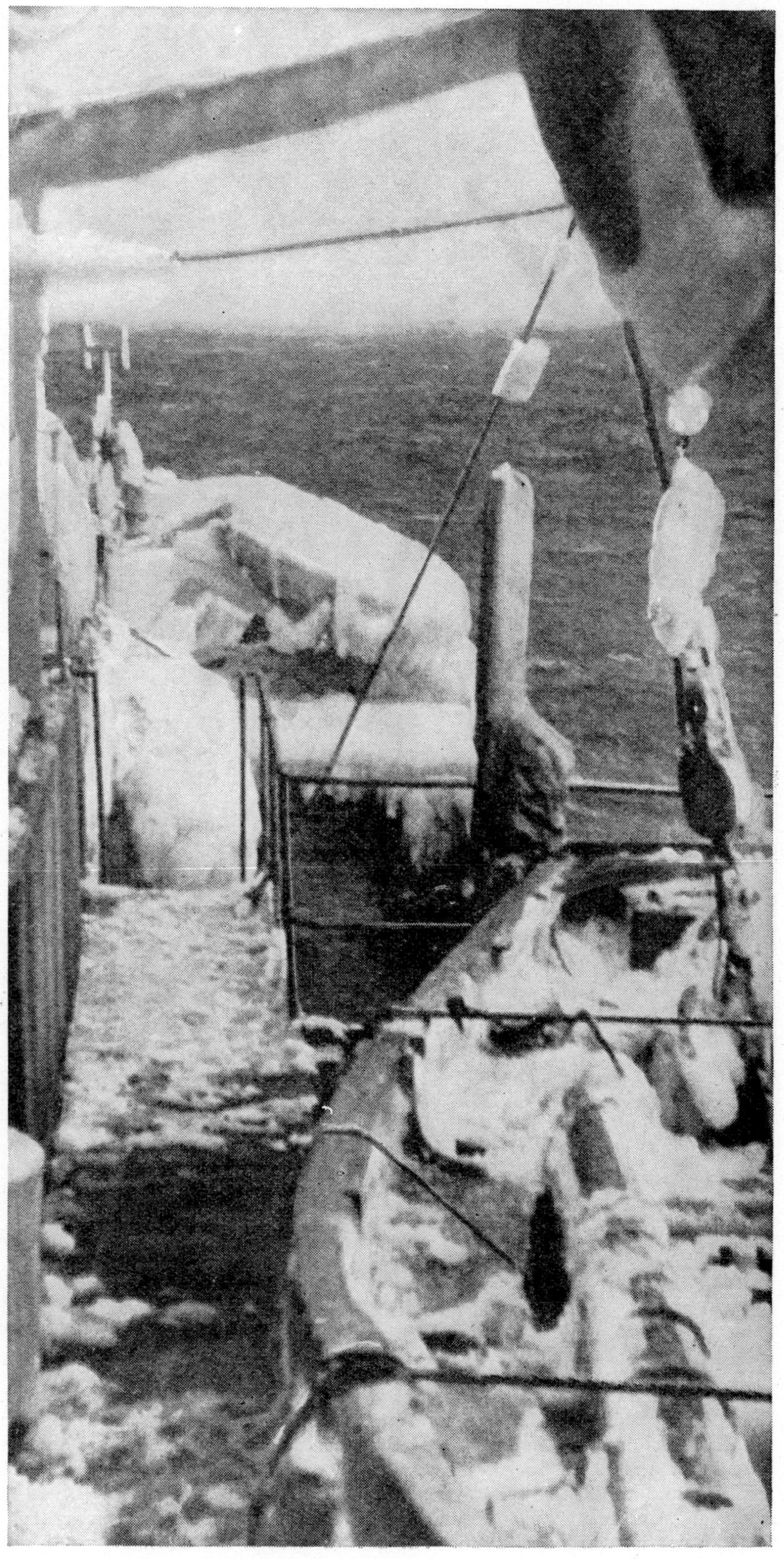

WINTER CONDITIONS ON THE ARCTIC CONVOY ROUTE. On 6 October diplomatic representatives of Great Britain, the United States and the U.S.S.R. signed a protocol covering deliveries of military equipment and war material to Russia. The bulk of British supplies had to be carried in convoys along the far northern route to Murmansk and Archangel, one of the most hazardous sea passages in the world. Apart from the menace of enemy submarines and shore-based aircraft, convoys had to fight their way through raging snow blizzards and seas infested with deadly ice floes, as the winter set in. These pictures of ice-coated decks on the ships of a Russia-bound convoy and escort give a vivid idea of what British seamen had to endure to keep our Russian allies supplied.

STREET FIGHTING IN STALINGRAD. On 18 October the Moscow radio declared that the decisive stage of the battle for Stalingrad had been reached. The enemy, using masses of infantry, tanks, artillery and aircraft, launched "all-out" attacks both in the northern factory area and in a southern thrust parallel to the Volga. But after bitter fighting, especially around the Red October and Red Barricade factories, they failed to gain any fresh ground and lost several thousand men and twenty-eight tanks. On 23 October German infantry detachments suffered heavy casualties in hand-to-hand fighting, and two enemy tanks which penetrated into the Red October works were destroyed. For several weeks the Germans made attack after attack in the northern

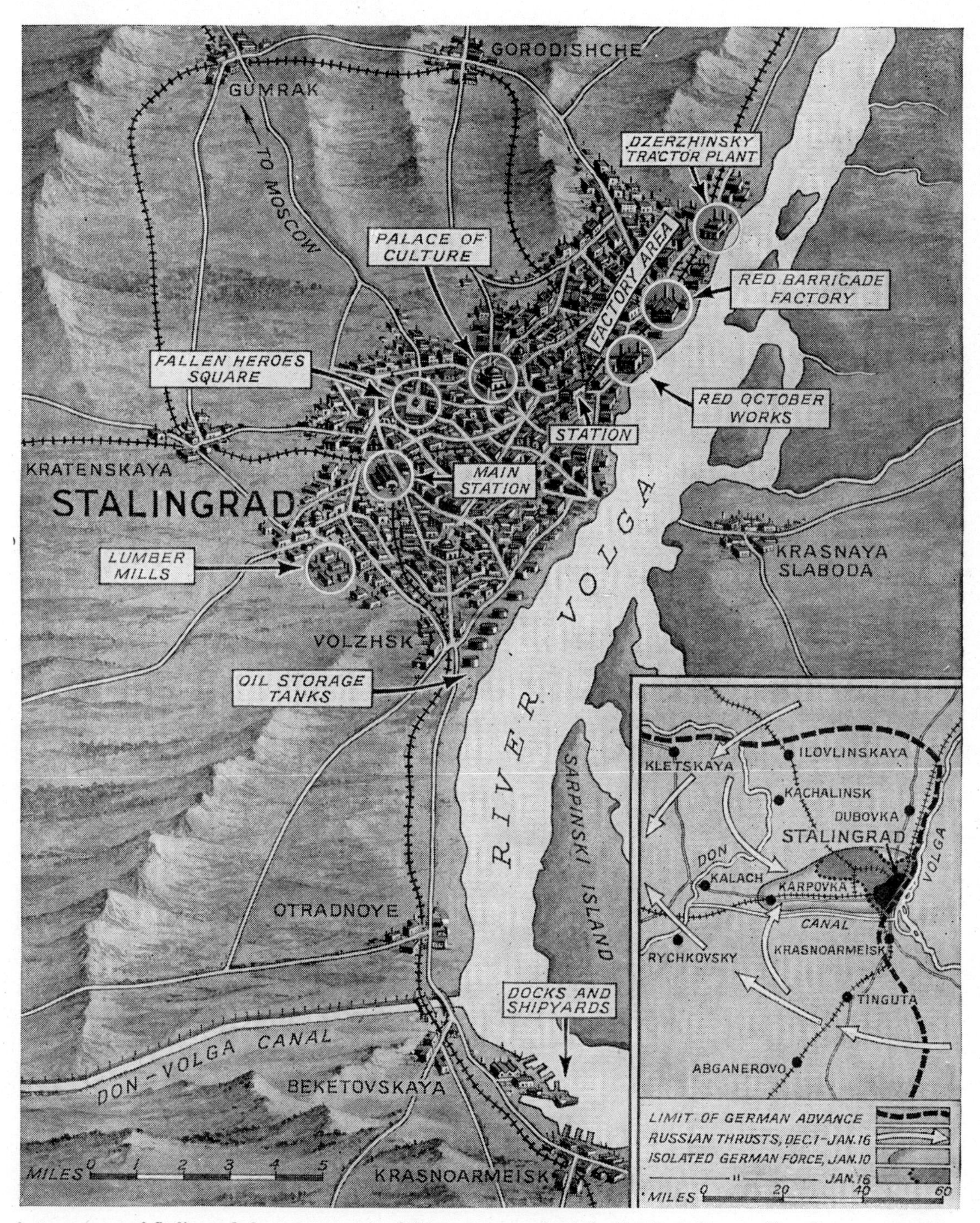

factory area of Stalingrad, but every one of them was repulsed by the Red Army. The German casualties mounted steadily day by day. By 8-10 November the Russian defenders had regained or destroyed many blockhouses and factory buildings which had been enemy strong points a few days earlier, and what advances the enemy was now able to make were weak and ineffective. Russian tenacity was, at long last, to gain its well-deserved reward. Seldom, if ever in history has a more bloody and prolonged hand-to-hand fight taken place. In the picture, left, Red Army riflemen are seen in action in a Stalingrad street. The map of Stalingrad, right, shows the farthest enemy advance into the city before the Red Army's smashing counter-attack on 19 November, 1942.

R.A.F. SMASH LE CREUSOT WORKS. On 17 October home-based bombers carried out the greatest unescorted daylight raid of the war to date. The target chosen for attack was the Schneider arms works at Le Creusot, about 170 miles south-east of Paris. The Schneider factories covered an area of more than 285 acres and were comparable in size with the German works of Krupps. Ever since the fall of France they had been engaged in the production of heavy and light guns, railway locomotives, rolling stock and other war material for the enemy. The raid was carried out by a force of ninety-four "Lancasters," led by Wing-Commander L. C. Slee, which attacked their targets from a record low level. A great weight of high-explosive bombs was dropped during an attack

which was concentrated into the space of only seven and a half minutes. So that casualties among the French civilian population should be as low as possible the "Lancasters" flew in singly to drop their bombs instead of in formation. At the same time other bombers attacked the Henri Paul transformer station, about five miles from Le Creusot, which supplied all the power to the Schneider plant. Despite the great risks involved in this daylight operation, necessitating a flight of some 800 miles, only one of the "Lancasters" failed to return to its base, although the bombers had no fighter escort throughout their attack. Great damage was caused to the huge armament works. The photograph, above, shows a number of the bombers flying low over a French town on their way to the target.

R.A.F. STRIKES AT ITALY'S WAR INDUSTRY

On the night of 22 October a powerful force of British four-engined bombers flew 1,400 miles across the Alps and back to drop a great weight of bombs, including many 4,000-pounders, on the Italian port of Genoa. Nearly twenty major fires were started all over the city, and R.A.F. pilots saw oil storage tanks and explosive dumps in the dock area blown into the air by direct hits. Another heavy attack was made on the city the following night when targets at Turin and Savona were also bombed. This was only the beginning of a sustained air offensive against the chief ports and manufacturing cities in North Italy, where Mussolini's war industry was almost entirely concentrated. The bombing was part of the Allied plan to smash the Italian war machine and also to hamper the Axis forces in Libya and Tripolitania while the Eighth Army was making its great advance westwards. Genoa, besides having vital arms factories, power stations and dock installations, was the chief port of supply for Rommel's armies. On 24 October a force of more than eighty home-based "Lancaster" bombers made the first daring daylight raid on Milan, attacking their targets from such a low altitude that many of the R.A.F. machines flew in below the level of the balloon barrage over the city to release their loads of bombs. Nevertheless, in spite of much lively opposition from the anti-aircraft defences, all except three of the British planes returned safely. The attack on Milan was continued after dark on the same day. For just as the "Lancasters" arrived back in Britain a stronger force of "Stirlings," "Wellingtons" and "Halifaxes" took off from their bases to raid the Italian city again. On the 7 November Genoa suffered its heaviest raid of the war so far when a great force of British bombers rained high explosive and incendiary bombs over a wide area of the city, leaving fires spreading rapidly among the warehouses and dock installations. Like many other cities in North Italy which were to feel the weight of R.A.F. blows in the weeks and months ahead, Genoa was obviously ill-prepared to meet these large-scale air attacks. The civil defence and fire-fighting organizations were thrown into such a state of confusion that they were quite unable to deal adequately with the many widespread fires and the dislocation of essential public services. The photograph shows loads of rubble collected from the devastated areas in Genoa being unloaded along the waterfront and thrown into the sea.

ANTI-U-BOAT WARFARE INCREASED

After the First Lord of the Admiralty had stated in Parliament in September that no fewer than 530 U-boats had been sunk or damaged since the outbreak of war, new and more deadly methods were taken against the enemy at sea in the following month, when successes in the Atlantic, the Mediterranean and elsewhere were much more encouraging. On 4 November the new Anti-U-boat Warfare Committee held its first weekly meeting in London to discuss new means of grappling with the peril at sea. This organization, marking a new phase in Allied sea warfare, was formed out of the Battle of the Atlantic Committee which had been set up by Mr. Churchill in February, 1941. The pictures show: above, the crew of a damaged Italian submarine surrendering to a British destroyer in the Mediterranean; bottom, left, a German U-boat returning to its concrete 'pen" inside the well-protected harbour at Lorient; bottom, right, the crew of another Italian submarine in the water awaiting their rescue by British ships.

BRITISH OFFENSIVE IN EGYPT BEGINS

The long-expected attack by the Eighth Army began in bright moonlight on the night of 23 October at El Alamein, following the heaviest gun barrage ever put up in the Western desert. For this preliminary softening of Rommel's deep defence lines the Allied artillery were ranged on a front of six miles with one gun to every twenty-three yards. For several hours a hell of fury was let loose on the enemy's positions before the Eighth Army, with powerful air, artillery and tank support, went forward to the attack. General Montgomery used entirely new tactics in this battle by making a frontal attack against an unbroken line of trenches and minefields. The first stages of the attack were carried out by British and Dominion infantry, who, by dawn on 24 October, had penetrated four miles through the gap in the enemy's advanced minefields. The enemy's main positions were successfully attacked at several points and many German and Italian prisoners were taken. Heavy fighting continued throughout the day and night while our troops consolidated their positions, and by the evening of 25 October the number of prisoners taken had mounted to 1,450. Meanwhile, the Allied Air Forces, working in perfect co-operation with the Eighth Army, kept up their non-stop blitz on enemy troop concentrations, landing-grounds, transport and supply lines. On the first day of the attack well over a thousand sorties were made by Allied bombers and fighters, dealing devastating blows on Rommel's communications and paving the way for the advance. On the night of 1-2 November, General Montgomery launched a great offensive with strong tank support on a 4,000-yard front fifteen miles west of El Alamein. Our infantry, fighting their way through minefields, barbed-wire and booby traps, had at last cleared a way for the armoured forces. All day long on 2 November the great tank battle raged at El Aqqaqir. This was the turning-point which led to the clearing of the enemy from Egypt and their pursuit into Libya. The picture shows a long line of British tanks moving up to the battle area

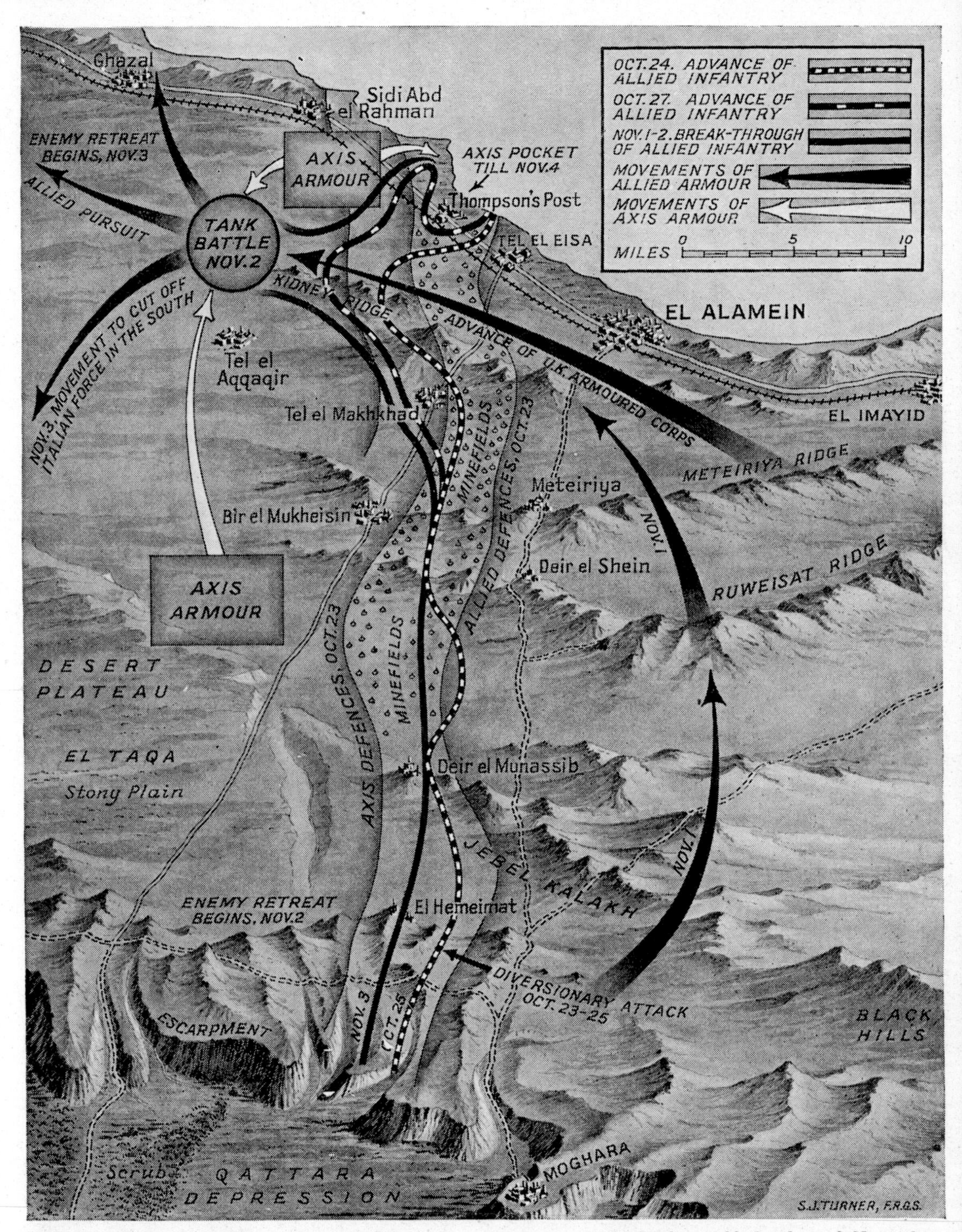

BATTLE OF EL ALAMEIN. This map shows the main phases of the battle on 23 October—3 November. Rommel anticipated that the Eighth Army would attack his centre, but instead the British struck against the strongest German lines in the north. Following the infantry-driven wedge in the enemy's minefield defences came the armoured break-through and the decisive tank battle on 2 November. This split the Axis armour in two, and on 3 November British infantry swung south to cut off the isolated Italian infantry divisions in the waterless desert.

Clearing "Hell Fire" Pass

ROMMEL CHASED FROM EGYPT. On 3 November the Eighth Army began the pursuit of Rommel's battered divisions towards Libya. Next day the Africa Korps was in full flight, leaving behind 13,000 prisoners and vast quantities of material. By 6 November Axis prisoners totalled 20,000 and the British had captured some 400 tanks, 350 guns and thousands of vehicles. After slight resistance Mersa Matruh was regained on 8 November and Sidi Barrani on 10 November. The coast road towards Sollum and the Halfaya Pass became choked by the retreating enemy, whose columns were thrown into hopeless confusion by the incessant strafing of Allied bombers. By 10 November the Eighth Army was established on both sides of Halfaya, a contingent of Dominion troops having moved up from the south. Large numbers of Axis troops were trapped between Halfaya and Sollum. On 11 November the Halfaya Pass was captured and over 1,100 prisoners, mainly Italians, fell into our hands. As the Axis forces retreated Italian engineers were detailed to blow up the coast road at Halfaya. It took great numbers of them four days and nights to finish the demolitions. Nevertheless, the Eighth Army's engineers replaced it within twenty-four hours. The photograph shows a party of New Zealanders at work.

NAVY BRINGS SUPPLIES ASHORE. Right from the first day of General Montgomery's advance at El Alamein the Royal Navy maintained the closest co-operation with the British forces on land. Between 24 October and 3 November, naval units, operating from Alexandria, carried out operations in the enemy's rear, shelling defences along the coast. Although the ships were attacked from the air they suffered no losses. With the reoccupation of Sollum and Bardia on 12 November, the Eighth Army had now won back several useful ports on the Mediterranean to which the Royal Navy could bring regular supplies. Fresh water was one of the major problems of warfare in this arid desert country, particularly on account of the speed of the British advance. But the Navy, rue to its tradition, helped to provide a solution. Soon after our troops had entered Sollum 33,000 barrels of water, each containing about 44 gallons, were brought ashore at Sollum with the aid of improvised landing craft. This picture shows some of the barrels being rolled on to the beach by naval ratings.

Destroying enemy supplies on land

ROMMEL'S SUPPLY LINES BATTERED. On 13 November the Eighth Army continued the swift pursuit of the fleeing Axis forces across Cyrenaica and reoccupied Tobruk and Gazala. All the time the Allied Air Forces maintained day and night attacks on the enemy's transport and supply columns with devastating effect. This was done without any opposition from the Luftwaffe which, in fact, was beaten out o. the skies even before the Battle of Egypt had opened. The pictures show: above, the accuracy with which one of Rommel's supply trains was attacked, and, below, the results of low-level strafing on an enemy railway track in the desert.

LIBYAN PUSH GOES ON

On 13 November South African troops under General Pienaar occupied Tobruk and reed hundreds of native soldiers who had been in German hands there for five months. Thus was avenged the loss of the 2nd South African division at Tobruk in Rommel's offensive of the previous summer. By the next day the Eighth Army had advanced to Tmimi, sixty miles beyond Tobruk, where the retreating enemy, heavily bombed and strafed by the Allied air forces, was unable to put up any delaying rearguard action. On 15 November the finest airfield in the Western desert fell into our hands by the capture of Maturba. During the next few days operations were slowed down by bad weather. Nevertheless, General Montgomery's forces made progress to the north and south of Benghazi. One of the R.A.F.'s heaviest attacks in the Western desert was made on the docks at Benghazi before its occupation by British and Dominion troops on 20 November. During the attack seven "Ju 52s" were shot down and many destroyed on the ground, while two ships were left burning. The pictures show: top, left, a British Bren carrier negotiating enemy barbed wire, and, top, right, a German tank crew surrendering to British infantrymen. Below is a remarkable picture of a desert sandstorm, one of many with which the Eighth Army had to contend during its advance.

Rapid British drive fro

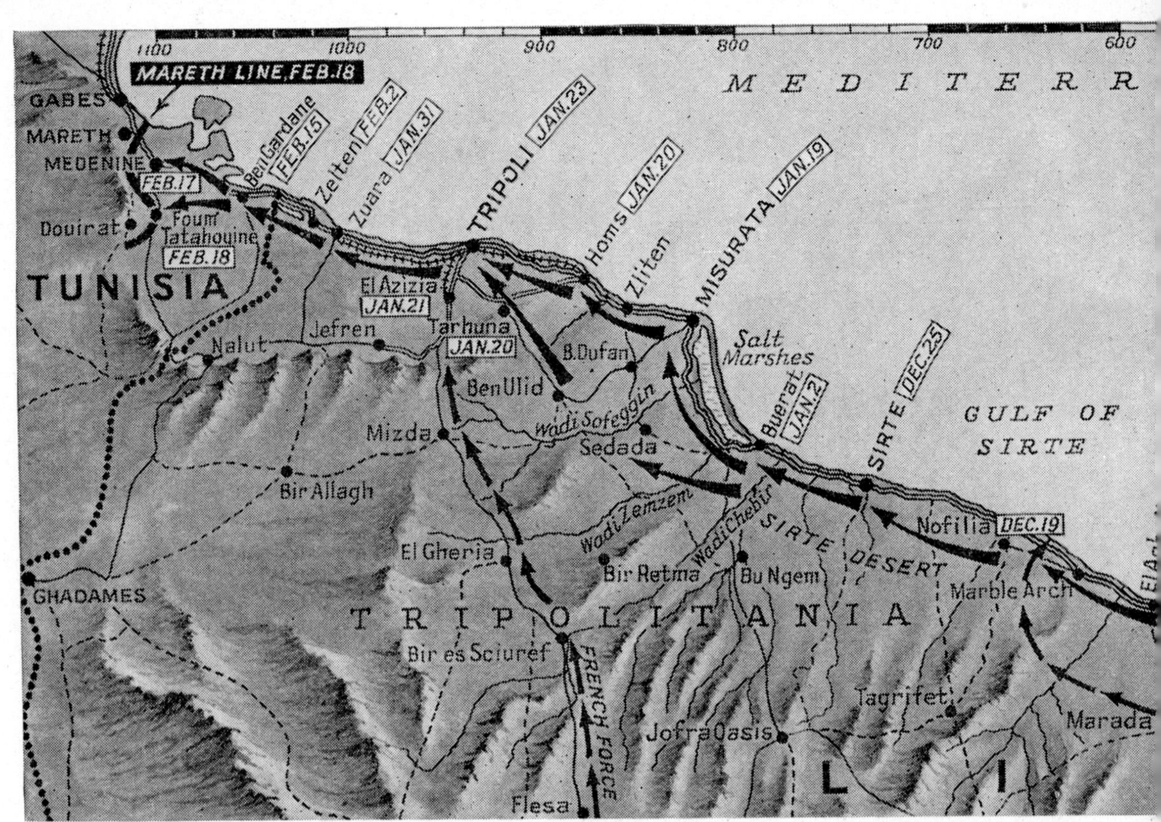

BATTLE FOR EL AGHEILA. After the recapture of Benghazi on 20 November the Eighth Army continued to pursue the Axis forces relentlessly towards El Agheila. Bad weather made the going very hard and the loosened sand after heavy rains seriously hindered the progress of British tanks and supply vehicles. These unfavourable conditions also restricted air activity for some days. Nevertheless, forward units of the Eighth Army maintained contact with the enemy's rearguards in the area around Jedabia, and this place was occupied by British troops on 23 November. Air operations were resumed on 26 November when a strong bomber force attacked the Axis landing ground at "Marble Arch" and started large fires among hangars and dispersed aircraft. During the lull

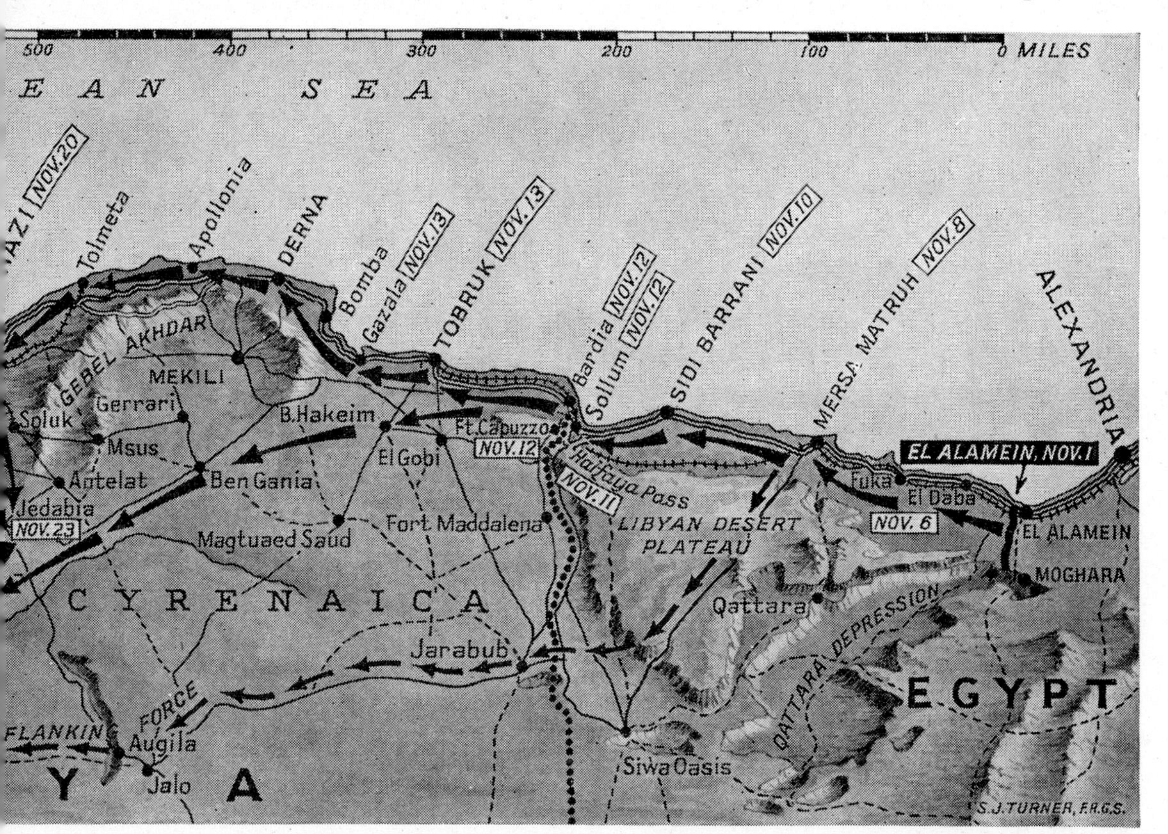

in the land fighting, General Montgomery concentrated his troops near El Agheila, where Rommel was expected to make a last stand before Tripoli. On 13 December the Eighth Army attacked in strength and occupied Rommel's main defences at Mersa Brega, east of El Agheila. Although El Agheila itself offered very good natural defences, the Africa Korps had begun its retreat westwards again even before the Eighth Army delivered the main attack. The map above shows details of the British advance from El Alamein to El Agheila, which was taken on 13 December, and the subsequent victorious drive to Tripoli and the Mareth Line inside Tunisia. The pictures below show the difficult conditions for our transport between Benghazi and El Agheila.

ALLIES LAND IN FRENCH NORTH AFRICA

Early on 8 November, a few hours after the first parties of the American Expeditionary Force had been put ashore at many points on the coasts of Algeria and Morocco, the world heard the news of the greatest combined military operation in history. In the statement issued from Allied headquarters it was revealed that the entire operations were under the supreme command o Lieutenant-General Dwight Eisenhower of the United States Army and were supported by powerful units o. the Royal Navy and Allied Air Forces. Steps were taken immediately to inform the French people, by radio and leaflets, of the landings and to assure them that the Allies sought no territory and had no intention of interfering with the French authorities in Africa. The landings were designed to forestall the occupation by the Axis powers of any part of North or West Africa, and to deny to the enemy a starting point from which a possible attack might be launched against the Atlantic seaboard of the Americas and the British West Indies. They also provided an effective second front for relieving the great pressure on the Russians and, moreover, were the first bold step towards the liberation of France and her Empire. Another important factor was the timing of the landings in French North Africa to coincide with the Eighth Army's offensive against Rommel in the Western desert. The outstanding initial success was due, not only to the perfect co-operation between the Allied orces, but also o the great secrecy which had been maintained. Mr. Churchill, in a speech to the House of Commons on 11 November, revealed that orders for the expedition to French North Africa had been issued at the end of July, 1942. A vast convoy of ships had to be assembled to carry tens of housands of troops and their fighting equipment to the landing grounds. This armada included more than 500 transports with about 350 protecting naval vessels. Powerful air cover was provided for the convoy all the time it was at sea and, despite the very great hazards of the route across the Atlantic and through the Western Mediterranean, all he ships arrived safely. The troops disembarked under cover o. darkness and were convoyed from the transports to the beaches in auxiliary .and ng craft. The picture shows part of the huge convoy a sea heading for North Africa.

SURRENDER OF ALGIERS. After the first landings on 8 November, the city of Algiers and its important airfields came under the control of the Allied forces. Sidi-Ferruch, twenty miles to the west, was also captured, while resistance put up by the coastal batteries at Cape Matifou was quickly overcome. Along the whole coast opposition by the Vichy forces was mainly weak and strategic points were gained as the Americans advanced

inland. In the Oran area the landing parties first captured places on either side of the city. By penetrating inland to a depth of several miles the Americans encircled Oran and captured three of its four airfields together with 2,000 prisoners. The city fell on 10 November to U.S. tank and infantry forces and thereby all Vichy resistance in Algeria ended. Above: Allied ships in Algiers harbour protected by a smoke screen.

ASSAULT ON CASABLANCA. On 10 November it was announced that British land and air forces were operating with the Americans in the North African campaign. The same day French warships which offered resistance in Casablanca harbour were bombarded and dive bombed by Allied warships and planes. Rear-Admiral Hewitt, commander of the U.S. naval forces, threw the whole of his fleet into the battle. An entire flotilla of French destroyers and lighter craft was wiped out, a French cruiser was hit and badly damaged, and the new 35,000-ton battleship "Jean Bart" was left in flames. Meanwhile the Allies continued their advance inland. On 11 November a conference was held at Algiers between Major-General Clark and Admiral Darlan, after which the latter issued a proclamation ordering all French land, sea and air forces to cease fighting against the Allies. The news was also given that members of the German Armistice Commission had been captured on 9 November by two British privates while attempting to flee from Algiers. The pictures show: above, transports moving inshore while U.S. Rangers await the order to transfer to landing craft; top, right, a landing-barge discharging troops; bottom, right, landing stores and equipment on a small beach to the west of Oran.

102
XM84

FIRST BATTLES IN TUNISIA. After the Allied landings in North Africa early in November the Germans seized control of Bizerta and Tunis and formed a strong defensive ring around them. On 15 November British and American advanced troops crossed the frontier into Tunisia. British paratroops were dropped at many key points, seizing aerodromes and taking prisoners. After preliminary tank and infantry clashes and the routing of an enemy mechanized column on 20 November, heavy fighting developed as the Allies advanced towards the

German fortified line west, south and east of Bizerta. On 27 November, after overcoming stiff enemy resistance, the British First Army occupied Medjez-el-Bab, thirty-two miles west of Tunis. On the following day our troops pressed forward, with strong air support, for another seventeen miles and entered the town of Tebourba. By the capture of Djedeida on 29 November, the First Army had cut the railway line between Bizerta and Tunis. The photograph shows vehicles and supplies for the British First Army being unloaded along the waterfront at Oran.

Red Army stand

FIGHTING IN THE CAUCASUS

Ever since August, 1942, the Germans had fought desperately to reach the oilfields of the Caucasus. After crossing the Kerch Straits from the Crimea they reached the Black Sea port of Anapa, twenty miles north-west of Novorossisk, on 1 September. Another enemy force had already penetrated the mountains protecting Novorossisk from the north. On 11 September, following a week of violent battles, the great naval base was evacuated by the Russians. Soviet Marines, co-operating with the Red Army and supported by the Black Sea Fleet, held the enemy's drive along the coastal road towards Tuapse. The Germans were unable to put the Russian Fleet out of action, despite its loss of important bases. Consequently, they were prevented from landing large invasion forces on this front. Meanwhile, the German armies advancing south to Tuapse through the mountains from Maikop made ittle progress. The most serious enemy advance was along the northern mountain slopes of the Caucasus towards the Grozny oilfield. This came within the Germans' grasp until, on 8-12 September, they were halted on the Terek River by the Red Army. The Germans then brought up large Alpine troop reinforcements to attempt an outflanking movement through Nalchik towards Ordzhonikidze at the end of the Georgian military highway. Little progress was made, and everywhere enemy attacks were repulsed with heavy losses. By 30 October the Red Army had to withdraw near Nalchik owing to the pressure of numerically superior enemy forces and the town was evacuated on 2 November. But the Russian positions on the Terek River held firm. It appeared that the Germans were trying to break through at Ordzhonikidze and gain control of the outlets to the Georgian and Ossetian military highways. By 5 November the advance beyond Nalchik was checked and the approaches to Ordzhonikidze held. The picture shows a Red Army patrol in the mountains

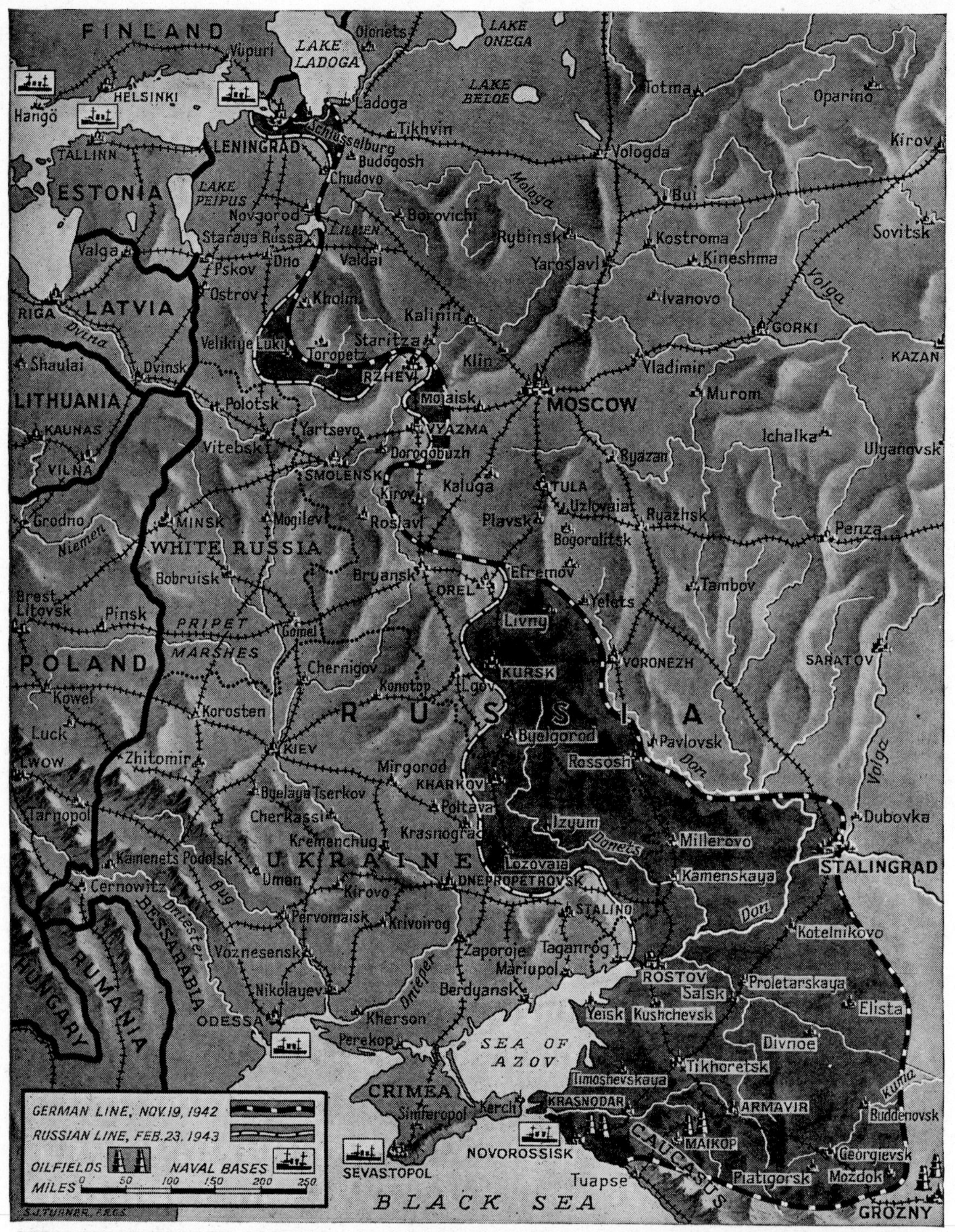

GERMANS RETREAT IN CAUCASUS. After weeks of fighting, the Red Army regained the initiative in the Caucasus on 19 November. Their decisive victory near Mozdok lessened the serious threat to the Grozny oilfield. Here the Germans suffered crushing defeat, losing 20,000 men killed and wounded. Booty captured by the Soviets included 140 tanks, 70 guns, 84 machine guns, and 2,350 lorries. The map, drawn by S. J. Turner, F.R.G.S., shows the extent of the German push and the line to which they were forced to retreat three months later.

RUSSIAN REINFORCEMENTS MOVE FORWARD. On 20 November the Russians, continuing their offensive in the Caucasus, repulsed four enemy counter-attacks and wiped out a whole battalion of crack Roumanian infantry in a sector to the south-west of Mozdok. In the neighbourhood of Ordzhonikidze the enemy were now in full retreat, abandoning one position after another with hardly a fight, while trying to retire into the cover of the mountain forests. The battered German divisions left behind thousands of dead and quantities of equipment and stores. Meanwhile, fresh Russian forces, trained for winter warfare, were sent from the east to strengthen the Red Army's powerful offensive on this front. The pictures show: above, a column of Russian infantry passing through a valley in the Caucasus Mountains, and, below, German soldiers reaching an important railway siding at Krasnodar, only to discover that all the oil installations had been set ablaze by the Russians.

FRENCH FLEET SCUTTLED AT TOULON. On 27 November German troops entered Toulon to seize the major part of the French fleet which lay in harbour there. But before they could reach the harbour the French naval commander, Admiral de Laborde, gave orders for all the ships to scuttle themselves. The captains stayed on the bridge until their ships went down, and many lost their lives. The scuttling of the French Mediterranean Fleet, in which 230,000 tons of naval shipping went to the bottom, was the greatest operation of its kind since the German

Fleet committed suicide at Scapa Flow in June, 1919. Among the warships destroyed were the 26,000-ton battleships "Dunkerque" and "Strasbourg," the old 22,000-ton battleship "Provence," the 10,000-ton cruisers "Algerie," "Colbert," "Foch," and "Dupleix," and the 7,600-ton cruisers "Jean de Vienne," "La Gal ssonnaire," and "La Marseillaise." Twenty-eight destroyers and twenty submarines were also sunk. The drawing, by Charles Cundell, gives a striking impression of the scene in Toulon harbour as the ships went down.

GERMANS COUNTER-ATTACK IN TUNISIA. By 1 December the most bitter fighting in Tunisia was centred around Mateur and Djedeida where the Germans launched a heavy counter-attack with intensive air support. At first the enemy failed to break up the First Army's thrust between Bizerta and Tunis, but further counter-attacks caused the Allies to fall back. By ceaseless dive bombing and repeated tank attacks the enemy made all-out efforts to dislodge the British advance units before General Anderson was able to bring his main forces up to the battlefront. The Allies were at a disadvantage owing to local German air superiority, because their own air strength had not yet been fully brought into action. On 4 December enemy forces recaptured Djedeida and held

it against attacks by British infantry and American tanks. Tebourba was evacuated by the British next day, when they retreated to entrenched positions overlooking the town in order to foil an enemy encircling movement. During these battles the Germans suffered heavy losses. Between 1-3 December no fewer than thirty-six of their tanks were destroyed and on 6 December a further twenty-one were knocked out. Meanwhile, Allied air strength continued to grow, although it was known that the Luftwaffe was also receiving reinforcements across the Mediterranean. The pictures show: left, a group of German parachutists in Tunisia taking cover as a shell burs' nearby, and, right, how the enemy rounded up local Arabs in gangs for forced labour on defence lines.

RUSSIAN ADVANCE CONTINUES

On 5 December the Red Army gained an important success when they recrossed the Don at several points in the Lower Don bend. Other Russian forces swooped down from the north and drove the Germans out of the towns of Sebretev and Parshin. So swift was the Red Army's advance on this front that by 26 December they had retaken Tatsyaskaya, an important road and rail junction 175 miles west of Stalingrad. Both Millerovo and the Voronezh-Rostov railways were now threatened. In the period 16-26 December the number of enemy prisoners rose by 6,300 to a total of 56,000 and war material captured included about 350 aircraft, 172 tanks and nearly 2,000 guns. The pictures show: top, left, German prisoners being marched away; bottom, left, Russian women soldiers being questioned after capture; bottom, right, Red Army men crossing the Don on collapsible floats.

DAYLIGHT RAIDS ON THE ENEMY. During December and early January daylight attacks of increasing force were made by British and American bombers on industrial targets in Germany and the occupied countries. On 6 December nearly 100 bombers of the R.A.F. made a concentrated attack on the Philips radio works at Eindhoven in Holland. This factory, the largest of its kind in Europe, was entirely engaged on production for the German armed forces. Large sections of the works were destroyed by fire. Another great raid was made on the steel works at Lille on 13 January by "Flying Fortresses." Over 150 tons of high explosives and a great weight of incendiaries were dropped on the main buildings within a few minutes and fierce fires were seen spreading over the whole area as the attackers flew away. The photographs show: top, left, clouds of smoke pouring from the Philips factory and, bottom, left, fires spreading over the Lille steel works after the attack. Above, a German "flak-train" used as an additional means of defence against the increased Allied air attacks over the Reich.

BRITISH AIR POWER IN THE DESERT. Following the routing of Rommel's armies at El Agheila on 13 December, the R.A.F. kept up almost incessant day and night attacks on the fast retreating Axis columns along the coastal road in Tripolitania. Whole lines of enemy transport and supply vehicles were wrecked, ammunition dumps were blown up, and airfields strafed from low levels. On 15 December day-long raids were carried out by British and American bombers on closely packed enemy columns about seventy miles west of El Agheila. At a place near "Marble Arch" blazing enemy vehicles caused a huge traffic block which delayed the retreating columns for many hours. Opposition from the Luftwaffe was negligible, but two enemy fighters were shot down. These far-reaching air attacks were made possible by the fine work of the R.A.F. Regiment in clearing advanced airfields so recently in enemy hands. At one airfield 2,000 mines were removed from a landing-ground within forty-eight hours to make it serviceable for Allied bombers. The pictures show: above, twisted remains o aircraft on an enemy landing ground in Libya, and, right, bullet-ridden Italian fighters and wrecked hangars at Castel Benito.

153
39

U.S. TROOPSHIP IS AVENGED

On 12 December, while carrying troops to a destination in the Pacific, the " President Coolidge " (former U.S. luxury liner of 21,000 tons converted into a troopship), hit an enemy mine off a small island in the Solomons group. Captain Henry Nelson, who was in command, rammed the stricken ship on to a coral reef. She slid off the reef, turned turtle and sank, but as a result of Captain Nelson's prompt action only two lives were lost, although there were 4,000 troops on board. The loss of the "President Coolidge" was offset by the outstanding victory achieved by the Royal Australian Air Force and the United States Air Force over the Japanese in the Battle of the Bismarck Sea, which provided a wonderful and unprecedented example of the annihilating effect of air power. A large and strongly escorted Japanese convoy, carrying reinforcements to New Guinea, was first sighted on Monday, 1 March, about 100 miles S.W. of Rabaul. It consisted of seven transports, of such importance that they were guarded by three cruisers and four destroyers. The reconnaissance plane which brought the news reported extremely bad weather, heavy clouds and storm. Allied aircraft set out to shadow the convoy, the largest yet seen in the Pacific. The next day, 2 March, it was larger still, having been reinforced, and now totalled twenty-two ships—ten warships and twelve transports. These were screened by large numbers of enemy planes. The Allied attack began after the enemy armada had been shadowed for nearly 200 miles. Bombers of the American Army Air Force, "Fortresses" and "Liberators," smashed their bombs down on the ships in a savage onslaught. One 10,000-ton transport was hit with five 1,000-lb bombs and left sinking; an 8,000-ton transport, split in two, sank almost at once. Through the next day "Beaufighters" joined in the attack. By now only two destroyers and three transports were left, and very soon afterwards all the twenty-two ships of the enemy armada had been sunk or were sinking. The 15,000 troops the transports carried were destroyed to a man. Fifty-five enemy aircraft were shot down. Picture shows troops scrambling down cargo nets and ropes from sinking "President Coolidge."

JAPANESE DEFEATED IN PAPUA. After a month of the most desperate fighting in the South-West Pacific, American troops captured Buna village on 14 December. During the night of 13-14 December a Japanese convoy attempted to land a relieving force from barges. But practically all the enemy were drowned or killed on the beaches by the heavy strafing inflicted by waves of Allied bombers. Fighting continued, however, in the small but strongly held Japanese salient round the Buna Mission, from which the enemy were not finally cleared until 2 January. The photographs show: top, left, American reinforcements landing on Papua; bottom, left, Australian infantry in a jungle action; above, the shore at Buna Mission strewn with the dead bodies of Japanese.

ADVANCE INTO TRIPOLITANIA

On 16 December the Eighth Army cut the retreating Afrika Korps in two by a brilliant outflanking movement at a place called Wadi Matratin, about sixty miles beyond El Agheila. This operation, which completely surprised the enemy, was actually planned by General Montgomery before the Battle of El Agheila, after British Intelligence officers had discovered a forgotten desert track running to the south and striking north to the coast road again along the Wadi Matratin. It was carried out by New Zealand troops under the command of General Freyberg, V.C. For three days the infantry advanced more than 100 miles over the desolate sand dunes and rocky wadis, supported by a strong force of artillery, tanks and armoured cars. The trapped Axis rearguard, which was entirely composed of German troops, fought desperately in its attempt to break through the British armoured ring. But although a few enemy troops and tanks managed to escape and join their main forces farther west, heavy punishment was inflicted by the New Zealanders. The enemy lost at least twenty tanks, thirty guns and several hundred motor vehicles. Five hundred Germans were taken prisoner. One of the most important results emerging from this action, according to a Cairo dispatch, was the capture or destruction of a very considerable amount of Rommel's motor transport and also appreciable numbers of his rearguard. On 18 December the Eighth Army, after mopping-up operations, continued its advance from Wadi Matratin and came to within thirty miles of Sirte, almost half-way between Benghazi and Tripoli. The remarkable action picture on the left shows a small forward party of Australian infantry with bayonets and fire-arms advancing in the desert through a protective smoke screen after being detailed to capture a German strong point on the way towards Tripoli.

WINTER ADVANCE IN THE CAUCASUS. On 25 December the Red Army launched a new thrust against the enemy south-east of Nalchik and recaptured Alagir and Krasnogorsk, thereby regaining the use of the Ossetian military highway. Next day Russian ski troops advanced thirty miles across the snow and wiped out an enemy salient which still menaced the Grozny oilfields. On 3 January, Mozdok, the important communication centre of

the Caucasus, was retaken in a surprise attack by Cossack Guards. With Mozdok in Russian hands again the Grozny oilfields were denied to the invader. The picture shows a company of Russian ski 'roops on patrol. These soldiers played an important part in the Red Army's winter offensive. Time and again they tricked the Nazis because they were equipped with white uniforms and hoods, making them invisible against snowy ground.

EIGHTH ARMY ADVANCES TOWARDS TRIPOLI

Continuing to advance through Tripolitania, the Eighth Army chased the dwindling Afrika Korps along the coast road. The retreating enemy columns suffered continuous bombing from the air by the powerful Western Desert air force. On 25 December British troops occupied Sirte without opposition, but to the west of this town air operations were curtailed for a time owing to the bad weather conditions and violent sandstorms. Beyond the Wadi Bei-el-Kebir the Eighth Army's sappers were busily engaged for several days clearing away mines and booby traps which the Germans had strewn over the roads in great numbers in order to delay our progress. On 5 January our forces entered Buerat-el-Hsun, about sixty miles west of Sirte where the coast road turns north along the salt marshes towards Misurata and Tripoli. After crossing the Wadi Zemzem on 14 January, Eighth Army troops encountered enemy rearguards at a point seventy miles from Misurata, but Rommel soon abandoned all his defensive positions in this area. Four days later Misurata was occupied without any opposition, by 20 January the Eighth Army had progressed along the coast beyond Misurata to the important defensive positions of Homs and Tahuna, and on the following day advanced British columns had entered the suburbs of Tripoli, whose capture was announced less than forty-eight hours afterwards. Meanwhile heavy day and night blows were delivered against Tripoli harbour and the great Axis airfield at Castel Benito on the outskirts of the city. The picture, left, shows British infantry advancing behind tanks in Tripolitania.

JAPANESE RESISTANCE ENDS AT BUNA

On 2 January Allied troops occupied the Government Station at Buna in New Guinea after shattering the Japanese defences there. By this victory the battle for Buna was virtually brought to an end after six weeks of the most bitter fighting amid swamps and jungles in one of the worst climates in the world. The last remaining point of enemy resistance in the Buna area was a small pocket to the west of the Giropa creek. There the Japanese continued to fight on desperately for several days until they were finally cut off by an American force which joined the Australians after the latter had taken the Government Station. Such was the ferocity of the fighting at Buna itself that on the last day 650 Japanese soldiers were killed. Enemy troops which tried to escape from the coast by swimming were attacked from the air by "Kittyhawk" fighters. By 3 January all organized resistance in the Buna area had ended, but Allied troops continued to mop up groups of isolated snipers. A few miles west of Buna small Japanese forces still showed resistance at Sananda Point, but owing to heavy rains and swollen swamps ground operations here were seriously hindered for many days. On 17 January, however, Allied troops cut the main road in two places behind the enemy's rear, less than 2,000 yards from the coast, and thereby split the remaining Japanese forces into three isolated groups. By next day two headlands on either side of Sananda Point had been captured and the enemy were now hemmed into a 500-yard strip of coast and a few isolated and surrounded pockets inland. Despite tropical rains and floods Allied progress continued and on 22 January the last remaining Japanese positions at Sananda fell and the reconquest of the Papuan part of New Guinea was completed. About 750 Japanese were killed in the final attack and a great quantity of military equipment and stores was captured. The picture shows Japanese killed and drowned on the beach at Buna Mission with a smashed landing boat in the background.

ALLIED CONFERENCE AT CASABLANCA. On 14 January the Prime Minister of Great Britain and the President of the United States met at Casablanca, in French Morocco, for important discussions on the future Allied operations in the war. They were accompanied by the combined Chiefs of Staff of the two countries and their expert advisers. This was the fourth wartime meeting of the two great Allied leaders. Although Marshal Stalin was invited to join in the talks he was unable to leave Russia owing to the offensive operations of the Red Army which he was directing. Nevertheless, he was fully informed of the decisions made, one of the objectives of which was to relieve pressure on the Russian forces. The far-reaching importance of this meeting in North Africa may be judged by the fact that it was the greatest gathering of Allied war chiefs called since the outbreak of the Second World War. Mr. Churchill left Britain on 12 January in the same "Liberator" which took him on his 14,000-mile trip to the Middle East and Moscow in August, 1942. President Roosevelt arrived in North Africa on 14 January after making the 5,000-mile flight across the Atlantic by "Clipper" plane. During the conference, which lasted ten days, the whole field o. the Second World War was surveyed in detail, and all Allied resources were marshalled for the more intense prosecution of the war by land, sea and air. Mr. Churchill and President Roosevelt and their respective staffs arr'ved at complete agreement regarding plans for offensive operations which were to be undertaken by the Allies against the Axis in the 1943 campaign. The conference also provided an opportunity for a meeting between the Fighting French leaders, Generals de Gaulle and Giraud. These pictures, taken at Casablanca, show: top, left, General Nogues (France) and General Patton (U.S.A.); bottom, left, President Roosevelt with Mr. Churchill; above, Generals de Gaulle and Giraud.

KITTY 40

BRITISH ENTER TRIPOLI. At 5 a.m. on 23 January the victorious Eighth Army entered Tripoli and the Union Jack was hoisted from a fort overlooking the harbour. Thus the last remaining capital of Mussolini's former empire passed into British hands, three months to the day since the offensive began at El Alamein. The final advance on the city came from three directions. Two columns of armoured units and New Zealand infantry pushed through the desert to the south, while the British infantry advanced from the east along the coast road. Most of the inhabitants of the city lined the streets as columns of British tanks, armoured vehicles and infantry filed into the main square from the suburbs. At midday General Montgomery received the official surrender of Tripoli from the Vice-Governor of Libya at a point just outside the city walls. Since the attack at El Alamein the Eighth Army had advanced 1,400 miles in ninety days to reach Tripoli, an average of nearly sixteen miles a day in most difficult country and often in bad weather. The pictures show: top, left, British tanks entering Tripoli; bottom, left, a party of Gordon Highlanders, with the harbour behind them; above, hoisting the British flag over the harbour.

LONGEST DESERT MARCH. On 30 January a mechanized force of Fighting French under General Leclerc reached Tripoli after a hazardous journey of 1,700 miles across the Sahara from the Chad territory of Central Africa. From their headquarters at Fort Lamy, near Lake Chad, they advanced into southern Libya, attacking many Italian outposts with the support of the French air force. On 6 January El Gatrun was stormed by a camel corps detachment under Captain Saruzac. Much booty and 177 Italian prisoners were taken. On 10 January General Leclerc's G.H.Q. announced the capture o: El Gatrun and Brach, another enemy outpost in the Fezzan oasis. The conquest of the Fezzan was completed on 12 January with the capture of Murzouk, the capital, and Sebha, the chief military base. On 27 January the Free French joined with another force under General Giraud at Ghadames to undertake further operations. The photograph shows General Leclerc talking to his men.

AXIS TROOPS CLEARED FROM LIBYA. Advancing still westwards from Tripoli the Eighth Army maintained contact with enemy rearguards and on 31 January occupied the port of Zuara, the last Italian town on the Tripolitanian coast. Meanwhile, advanced British patrols had already crossed the frontier into Tunisia to the south of the coastal road. On 2 February a fifteen-mile advance was made from Zuara to the village of Zelten, beyond which artillery duels were exchanged with the Axis forces withdrawing towards Pisada, only twelve miles from the Tunisian frontier. For the next two weeks progress was slower and operations on land were reduced to patrol activity until, on 15 February, the Eighth Army occupied Ben Gardane and its big airfield and began the advance towards Medenine and the Mareth Line. The photographs show: above, British 6-pounder anti-tank gun in action; and below, British infantry moving to capture an enemy strong point under cover of a damaged German tank.

GREAT ATLANTIC CONVOY BATTLE. On 18 March the Admiralty issued the account of one of the greatest winter battles of the Atlantic between a pack of U-boats and convoy escorts. The battle, which lasted for three days and nights in February, was fought out by British, U.S., and Fighting French escort ships, together with "Liberator" and "Sunderland" aircraft. The convoy did not escape without loss, but heavy damage was inflicted on the U-boats, three of which were sunk for certain and many others probably sunk. The picture on left shows

some of the survivors from a torpedoed ship being assisted aboard a rescuing vessel. The picture above shows the rescue of three British seamen from a raft on which they had lived for eighty-three days before being sighted and picked up by a U.S. Navy patrol boat. Two other companions had died on the raft and were buried at sea. The three castaways who survived had lived—or existed—for almost twelve weeks on fish, birds and rain-water; through hunger, thirst and long exposure to the weather they were reduced down to mere skin and bone.

Rapid construction of

NEW ROAD TO TOKYO. The U.S. State Department announced on 18 March, 1942, a Canadian-U.S. agreement for the construction, under the auspices of the Joint Defence Board, of the Alaska Highway linking the Continental United States with Alaska via British Columbia and Yukon. Work on America's "Burma Road" was begun at once and despite climatic and physiographic difficulties, 10,000 soldiers and 6,000 civilian workers under the direction of the U.S. Public Roads Administration pushed the construction work ahead at the rate of eight miles a day, bridging some 200 streams and laying the twenty-four foot wide roadway over mountain ranges, rivers and bogs. Intended to be in use by the end of the year, the highway was designed to be one of the most important lines of communication for reinforcing Allied forces in the Pacific, as well as to carry supplies to Russia and China with practically no risk. The picture above, gives some impression of the obstacles which had to be blasted from the path of the highway. Those on the right show: above, the highway in use at a point where transport drivers may obtain rest and refreshment on the way; and below, another section of the road driven through virgin forest.

ALLIES ON THE OFFENSIVE IN PACIFIC. The importance which the Japanese had attached to the Solomons, and especially to the island of Guadalcanal, where their construction of bases for the intended attack upon Australia was interrupted by the U.S. landing in August 1942, was revealed by the repeated attempts they made between then and February 1943 to regain control of the island. The strongest of these attempts, launched regardless of losses, involved the occupying U.S. forces and their protecting air and naval units in some of the toughest fighting of the whole Pacific campaign before it was finally announced on 9 February from Tokyo that Japanese troops had been evacuated from Guadalcanal. The pictures show: top, left, U.S. marines engaged in the task of mopping-up the island during the final offensive on Guadalcanal which was launched on 15 January; below, a command car of the American Army being ferried across a jungle river. Above, American troops in action on a gun site.

U.S. VICTORY ON GUADALCANAL. On 10 February it was announced from Washington that the whole of Guadalcanal Island was under American control. For six months it had been the scene of heavy fighting between the U.S. forces and the Japanese. The loss of this vital Pacific base was a severe defeat for the enemy. The Henderson airfield, which the Japanese had almost completed when U.S. marines landed on Guadalcanal in August, 1942, was intended as an air base for the invasion of Australia. The campaign cost the enemy 75,000 men, 800 aircraft and 166 warships and transports. During the final American offensive, which began on 15 January, U.S. troops killed more than 6,000 of the enemy, captured 130 prisoners and vast quantities of material. The pictures show: above, an American landing barge at Guadalcanal and, right, troops bathing on the island.

Bestial Nazi policy of

NAZI TERROR IN POLAND

On 9 July the Polish Government in London issued a statement describing the pitiable fate of Poles and Jews under the terror regime of the Nazi occupying forces. Within the past year, declared the Polish Deputy Premier, the number of Poles and Jews murdered had increased to 400,000, and in the months following Himmler's visit to Warsaw in March, the Gestapo had intensified their terror severely. The setting up of the ghetto in Warsaw in 1940 was later followed by the establishment of similar colonies in practically every Polish town and village. The Jewish deathrate in Warsaw alone was estimated at 6,000 weekly, and exhaustion, starvation and disease were systematically exterminating the Jewish population. The totally inadequate supplies of food for the inhabitants of these ghettos led to smuggling on a large scale, and the Germans themselves participated in this illicit trading. The consequences of this privation were particularly tragic during winter months, when scores of corpses were collected from the streets of the ghetto every day. The pictures below and above, right, among the first to reach this country, reveal something of the desolation and misery in which inhabitants of the Warsaw ghetto eked out their precarious existence; above, left, a grim cameo of the New Order in Poland shows Polish peasants lined up awaiting the execution squad. The man on the left of the picture is one of the many Polish priests against whom the Nazi terrorists vented their brutal wrath.

KURSK AND KHARKOV RECAPTURED. Immediately following the expulsion of the enemy from Voronezh the Red Army advanced rapidly for nearly forty miles on a broad front and liberated some 200 inhabited places in this area. These included the vital railway junction of Kastornaya and the town of Novy Oskol, both of which were heavily defended and fell only after bitter hand-to-hand fighting in the streets. On 4 February further gains in this sector brought the Russians to within thirty miles of Kursk which was encircled by them on three sides. This great German bastion was captured on 8 February after tremendous tank and infantry battles, and its loss endangered the whole German position in south Russia. Meanwhile, on the Donetz front farther south, fighting raged on the outskirts of Kharkov, the capital of the Ukraine. Despite the most stubborn German resistance by troops which included the "Adolf Hitler" tank division, the Russians, supported by great formations of dive bombers, smashed their way into the centre of the city on 16 February. Picked SS. troops, rushed from France to Kharkov only two weeks previously, were crushingly defeated and thousands of them were slain. The pictures show: above, aftermath of battle in a Russian village; right, German troops firing the homes of Russian peasants.

GERMANS DRIVEN FROM ROSTOV AND VOROSHILOVGRAD. On 14 February, after several days of violent house and street fighting, the Red Army recaptured the vitally important city of Rostov-on-Don for the second time. The renowned Cossack Guards Division, under the command of Col.-Gen. Malinovski, led the final and decisive assault against the city from the south-west bank of the Don. Rostov had been in the enemy's hands for practically six months. On the same day General Vatutin's forces won another great victory with the reoccupation of the industrial city of Voroshilovgrad after a furious battle which raged without interruption for forty-eight hours. During this battle the Red Army had to force a way through some 3,000 blockhouses and an elaborate network of anti-tank traps which the Germans had built during their occupation. The arrival of the Red Army brought shouts of joy from thousands of Russian peasants, many of whom had suffered incredible hardship under the hated invader. The pictures show: left, peasants returning to Rostov after exile; above, a Russian family mourning a relative killed by the Germans; below, some of the tragic refugees awaiting return to their homes.

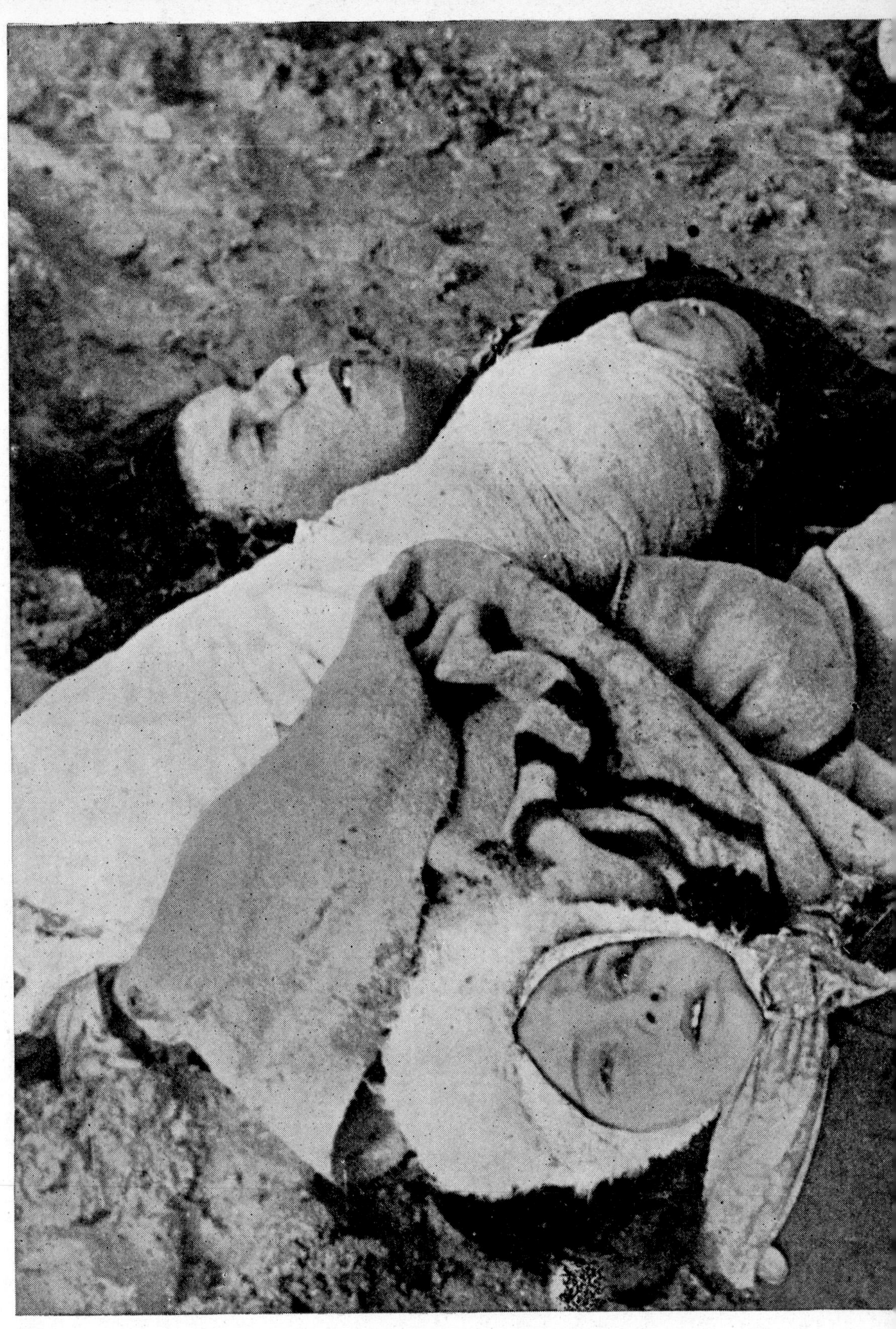

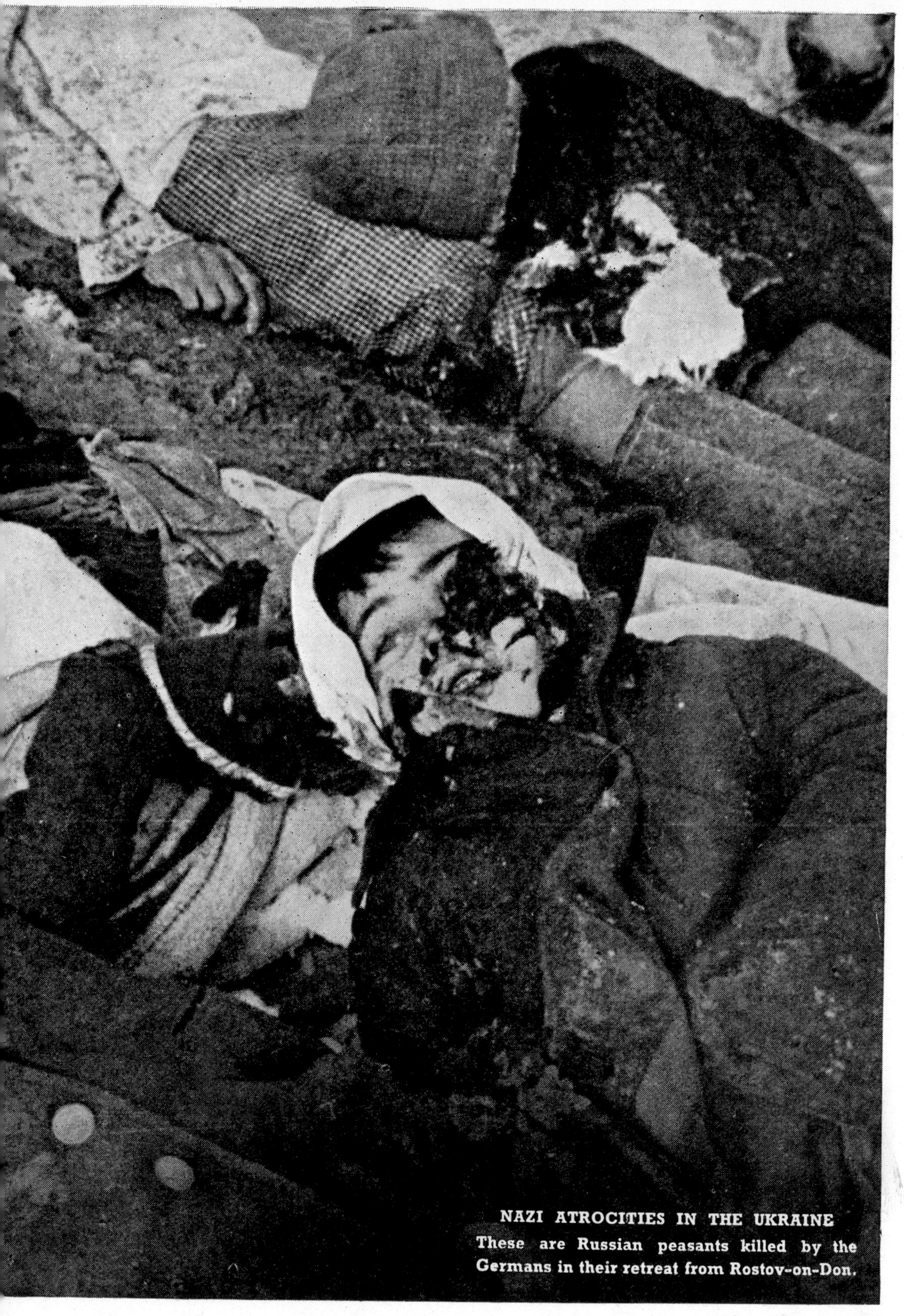

NAZI ATROCITIES IN THE UKRAINE

These are Russian peasants killed by the Germans in their retreat from Rostov-on-Don.

GROWING SUCCESS AGAINST U-BOATS. During the most critical period of the war at sea the enemy employed packs of U-boats to lurk in the path of Allied convoys. These new methods of the Germans, however, were successfully countered and the 600-mile danger gap in the Atlantic became less hazardous. The great strain under which U-boat crews worked is evident from the picture, right; which shows a crew waiting in suspense, listening to depth charges. The picture above shows an Allied destroyer about to drop its depth charges.

U.S. TROOPS FALL BACK IN TUNISIA. On 14 February, while the Eighth Army was pushing forward to Medenine after capturing Ben Gardane, the Germans launched a strong attack against the relatively lightly held American lines in the central part of Tunisia. The attack was delivered by a German armoured division in two columns. Supported by masses of fighter aircraft and dive bombers, the Germans quickly overran the advanced American positions and completely isolated some artillery and infantry units. Counter-attacks somewhat delayed the enemy's advance, but Axis reinforcements were brought up in very strong force with the result that the U.S. troops were compelled to evacuate the Gafsa Oasis and also three of their forward airfields—one at Sbeitla and two at Telepte. After four days of fierce fighting the Americans were pushed back about thirty-five miles from the advanced positions they had previously held. The pictures show: top, left, the American-built "Priest" gun-howitzer in action; bottom, left, troops moving up through the enemy barrage; above, a camouflaged British gun.

DESPERATE FIGHTING IN TUNISIA. On 21 February, having advanced thirty miles since they moved out from the Faid Pass, the Germans pierced the new shorter line held by the U.S. forces with a heavy Panzer attack. Thereafter they increased their pressure, and their mechanized and infantry columns made three strong assaults against Sbiba, Thala and towards Tebessa. The strongest attack, made with over seventy tanks and infantry, brought them to within a few miles of the key mountain town of Thala. British tanks and Guards units were sent as reinforcements. After desperate fighting the Allies succeeded in holding the Axis thrust, inflicting severe casualties and taking prisoners. On the first day a score of enemy tanks were knocked out. The next day the British brought into action for the first time a number of 40-ton " Churchill " tanks, and these inflicted considerable losses on the enemy. In one of these tank battles nine "Churchills" took on fourteen German tanks and destroyed four of them. Only one of the British tanks was lost. On 23 February the Germans were forced to withdraw. Allied success in recapturing the ground they had lately lost was largely due to heavy attacks by their combined air forces from bases far in the rear. The pictures show: above, British infantry attacking; right, shell bursting on German tank.

GERMAN ATTACKS REPULSED IN NORTHERN TUNISIA. On 26 February, while the enemy was hastily withdrawing from the Kasserine Pass, a heavy attack was launched against the British First Army in the north. No fewer than six separate attacks were made with 5,000 troops, including parachutists, with strong tank support. All of them, however, were repulsed and the enemy suffered a major defeat. More than 400 German prisoners were taken and many of their tanks and heavy guns knocked out. Nevertheless, the enemy continued to attack

on an eighty-mile front from Cape Serrat to Jebel Mansour, south-east of Bou Arada. Again he was thrown back at every point with heavy losses in men and material. In particular, the "Churchill" tanks inflicted serious punishment on the enemy's armoured columns. By 2 March the British forces had regained all the important points and the enemy, having suffered such grave casualties, reduced the momentum of his attacks. The picture shows British troops, with transport and light armoured cars, crossing a ford in Northern Tunisia.

INCREASED AIR BLOWS AGAINST NAZI WAR INDUSTRIES. On 1 March a heavy raid on Berlin (the heaviest which the German capital had experienced since the outbreak of the war) heralded a month of great Anglo-American air operations over Germany and the enemy-occupied lands of Europe. The offensive was kept up by night and by day, almost without pause, and the attacks were nearly all on a very large scale and highly concentrated. The chief armament-making cities, railway centres, ports and U-boat bases of the Reich all felt the weight of the renewed onslaught. It was the result not only of much-increased aircraft production in the British Isles, but also of the building-up of a vast American bomber force on this side of the Atlantic. The photograph above was taken during a daylight attack by "Flying Fortresses" on industrial targets at Rotterdam on 4 March. Bombs are to be seen falling, while another bomber makes its run at a lower level.

GREAT RAID DAMAGE AT ESSEN. Two of the most devastating air blows against Germany during March were aimed at the famous Krupps armament factories at Essen. These raids were carried out by strong forces of bombers on the nights of 5-6 March and 12-13 March and on both occasions extensive damage was done. On the last of these two Essen raids the attack was so powerfully concentrated that in less than forty minutes more than 150 4,000-lb. bombs and a great weight of incendiaries were dropped. A large section of Krupps' main buildings and workshops was destroyed and vital parts of the organization were put out of action for a considerable time. Many of the fires started were still ablaze twelve hours after the attacking aircraft had left. The photograph above shows the result of the raid in detail: (A) light railway shop ; (B) sheet metal shop ; (C) sheet metal works ; (D) brass press shop ; (E) warehouses adjoining light railway shop ; (F) press shop.

RUSSIA'S MIGHTY STRUGGLE. On a continuous front of over 1,000 miles Russia's fight against the invader never slackened in its fierce intensity. The German hope that the spring thaw would slow down the Red Army's advance proved unfounded. On 3 March the Germans were driven out of Rzhev (140 miles north-west of Moscow) with losses of 2,000 killed, and of booty including 112 tanks, 78 guns, and over 1,000 railway coaches. Rzhev had been so well fortified that to capture it by flank or frontal assault had been thought impossible; but the German commander, knowing that the Russians were grouping for a gigantic offensive, decided to evacuate the town. To hinder pursuit the Germans dynamited the bridges over the Volga. Advancing in the Northern Ukraine, Soviet troops had successes, capturing Lgov, fifty miles west of Kursk, and Dmitriev, thirty miles north of Lgov. On 12 March the Russians stormed Vyazma, and continued their drive towards Smolensk, the biggest German base in Russia. In the battles for Vyazma German losses were 9,000 killed. Pictures: above, the path of the Nazi retreat; top, right, Germans retreat through the snows ; bottom, right, Russian troops with machine guns on sledges.

CHINA ON THE OFFENSIVE

On 15 March the Chinese High Command announced a great victory on the Yangtse River front to the west of Hankow. A few days earlier more than 20,000 Japanese troops crossed the river in eight columns ready to launch an offensive towards Hankow. On 13 March, however, a general Chinese counter-offensive was begun, and after less than two days fighting the enemy was flung back in disorder and full retreat. Several places of strategic importance were recaptured in the province of Hupeh. This splendid victory showed that even after six years of brutal warfare the spirit of China's fighting forces was still high despite their isolation from the Allies, their serious lack of equipment and widespread famine among the civilian population. Nevertheless, in the spring of 1943 Generalissimo Chiang Kai-shek had some 5,000,000 fighting men under his command and another 15,000,000 men standing in reserve, trained and awaiting equipment. Nearly another 20,000,000 had received preliminary militia training. The great bulk of these Chinese armies was recruited from the peasant classes. This, in fact, was a source of their strength. For, being bred in the countryside, every man was well acquainted with the terrain in which he had to fight and was tough enough to cover the distances involved in the campaigns against the enemy. Since the Japanese began what they called the China "incident" the Chinese had made rapid strides with the development of their own war industries. As the "incident" approached its seventh year there were nearly 2,000 arms factories in parts of the country remote from enemy attack with thousands of trained women to work in them. The picture shows supply barges on the Yangtse River at Chungking.

Allied armoured force

BATTLES OF THE TANKS

In the Tunisian fighting the armoured divisions of both sides played a considerable part, and their support was indispensable to secure the full exploitation of any break through of opposing forces. On 6 March, the enemy made a heavy assault on British positions in Southern Tunisia with infantry and tanks. It failed signally. The enemy forces were compelled to withdraw towards the hills to the north of Medenine, and in one day's fighting thirty-three Axis tanks were destroyed without a single British tank being lost. Two days later enemy tanks captured by the British totalled fifty. At the end of February the important Kasserine Pass, which had seen much bitter fighting when it had been taken from the Allies by a very heavy Panzer attack a week earlier, was successfully cleared of the enemy and was once again in Allied hands. British and American infantry, supported by tanks, forced this enemy withdrawal. Among the prisoners who surrendered were many Italians. As the Eighth Army advanced and the number of enemy prisoners in our hands increased, the ratio of captured Italians to Germans was, on many occasions, found to be six to one, showing that the Germans had no compunction in deserting the soldiers of Italy, then their ally. The pictures on these pages show some incidents during this stage of the fighting in Tunisia: top, British tank crews mounting before an advance against enemy positions ; bottom, hundreds of war-weary Italian soldiers surrendering to the Eighth Army.

BATTLE OF THE MARETH LINE. On the night of 20-21 March the Eighth Army began a full-scale attack on the Mareth Line along a six-mile front between the sea and the Medenine-Gabes road. After thirty-six hours of fierce hand-to-hand fighting all preliminary objectives had been gained and British infantry, strongly supported by masses of tanks and aircraft, had driven a wide bridgehead into the north part of the line between Mareth and Zarat. As at El Alamein, General Montgomery delivered a frontal assault against the enemy's most vital sector and

strengthened this assault by heavy artillery attack and air bombardment. During the first phase of the operations 1,700 prisoners, nearly all of them German, were captured. For some days bitter and bloody fighting ensued and the enemy suffered heavy casualties. On 28 March the Eighth Army captured Mareth, Toujane and Matmata after overcoming strong enemy rearguard opposition and the entire Mareth Line fell into our hands. The photograph shows a section of British artillery shelling the Mareth defences just before the opening stages of the battle.

CROSSING THE WADI ZIGZAU. In order to reach their preliminary objectives in the Mareth Line on 20-22 March, British infantry columns had to fight their way across the rocky precipices of the Wadi Zigzau in the face of bitter opposition from the enemy. This wadi was the toughest natural obstacle the Eighth Army had encountered since the earliest days of their advance from Egypt. Yet Royal Engineers managed to bridge it under fierce enemy fire. The picture shows a British casualty being treated at one of the wayside dressing-stations in the Wadi Zigzau.

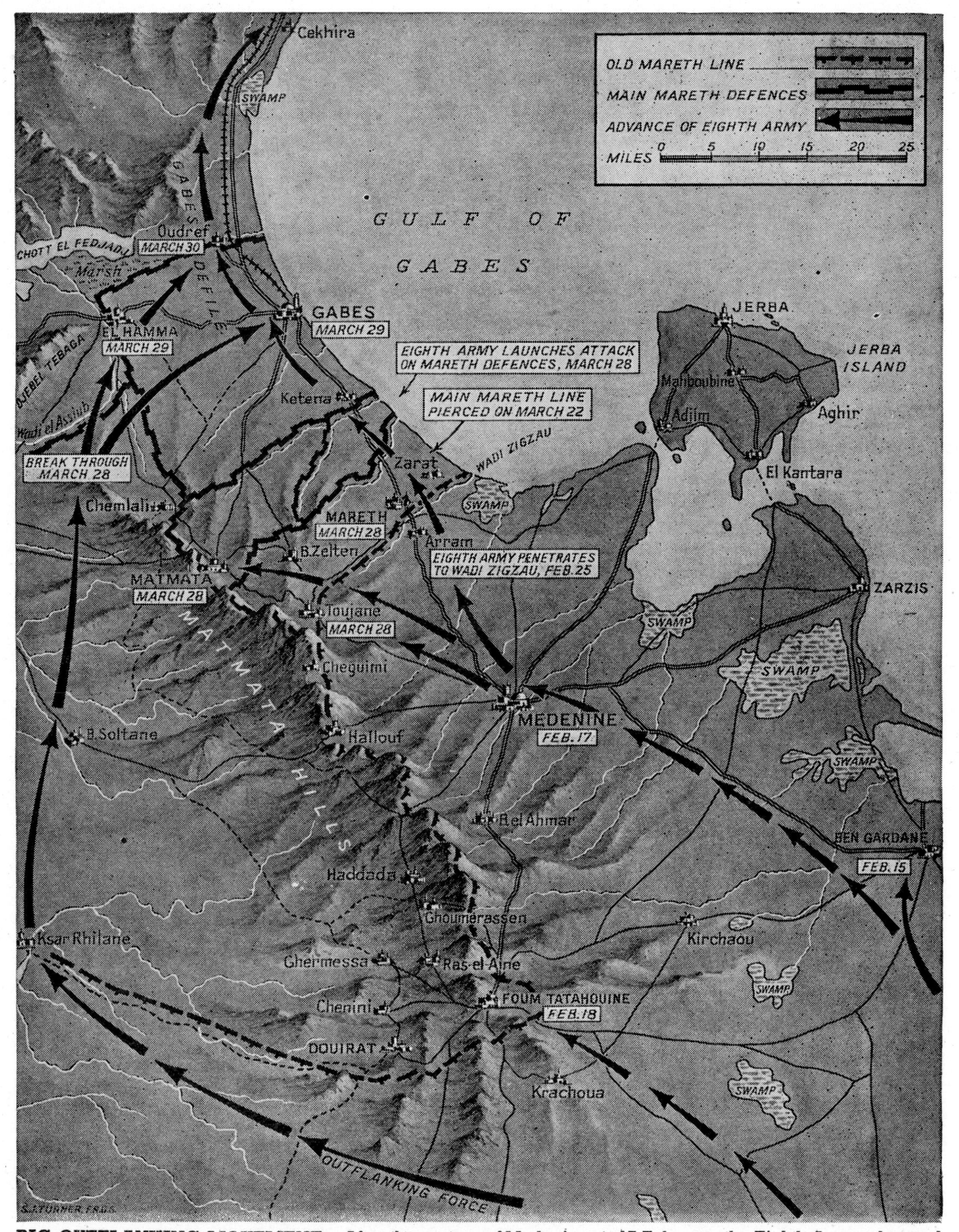

BIG OUTFLANKING MOVEMENT. After the capture of Medenine on 17 February the Eighth Army advanced to the Wadi Zigzau, a deep gorge forming part of the Mareth defence system. It proved to be such a tough obstacle that General Montgomery sent a wide outflanking force round the south of the Matmata Hills. On 28 March this outflanking force broke through strong enemy defence positions along the Wadi el Assiub. Meanwhile, our forces in the coastal sector occupied the whole Mareth Line, where the German position had been weakened.

AIR SUPPORT FOR THE EIGHTH ARMY. Before the Eighth Army's main attack on the Mareth Line, Axis forces in the Mareth-Gabes-Maknassi triangle suffered the heaviest air blows since the North African campaign began. For the first time the Western Desert and Tunisia air forces co-operated in this devastating assault. While fighters and light and medium bombers kept up a non-stop blitz on enemy airfields, transport and troop concentrations, night bombers attacked enemy bases in Sicily and Italy, and also shipping in the Mediterranean. On 30 March German resistance at El Hamma was finally broken by R.A.F. "tank-busters" which bombed enemy tanks and gun positions for nearly three hours without pause. The pictures show: above, laying wire " blankets " on a desert airfield; top, right, R.A.F. " Baltimores " on the way to raid enemy transport; bottom, right, result of a raid.

BATTLE OF AKARIT

The Eighth Army in Tunisia lost no time after its victory at Mareth. Only eight days after it had successfully broken the Mareth line it gained a new victory. In the pitch darkness of a moonless night, on 6 April, General Montgomery's main forces attacked the strongly fortified position of Akarit, north of Gabes, and battered their way to success after heavy and bitter fighting. The advance of the British and Indian infantry was preceded and covered by a terrific artillery barrage—the heaviest yet known in Southern Tunisia—from 500 guns. Within a few hours General Montgomery's troops wore down the enemy's determined resistance, captured the two key hills, Djebel Roumana and Djebel Fatnassa, on each side of his positions, and forced a gap in the enemy's line enabling our armoured forces to pass through. Fierce counter-attacks by the enemy were successfully repulsed, and by nightfall British tank squadrons had reached open country and were in pursuit of the retreating enemy. Six thousand prisoners were taken as a result of the first day's operations, and this fresh success by the Eighth Army enabled its troops to link forces with the Second U.S. Army Corps at Djebel Chemse, east of El Guettar. Most of the prisoners taken were Italians. Following up this success, the Eighth Army pushed forward along the coast, and on 8 April reached Cekhira, overlooking the Tunisian plain, an advance of fifteen miles from the Wadi Akarit line. It was now evident that the Afrika Korps was in full retreat. The fleeing enemy columns were harassed remorselessly by heavy and continuous air attack by bombers and fighter bombers of the Tactical Air Force. These wrecked or damaged great numbers of tanks and transport vehicles on the northern roads to Sfax, which British troops reached on 10 April, having covered over fifty miles since the attack on Akarit began. The number of prisoners captured had now mounted to 10,000. The picture on the right shows a dead German beside his wrecked gun.

EIGHTH ARMY STRIKES NORTH AGAIN. After it had captured the port of Sfax on 10 April, the Eighth Army pushed on northwards over most difficult marshy country which the enemy had sown profusely with mines and booby traps. Nevertheless, in spite of these obstacles the advance was rapid over the eighty-mile stretch to Sousse, which was entered on 12 April. Sousse, the third largest port in Tunisia, was occupied without opposition, although the enemy had destroyed all the port and dock installations and the town's electricity and water supplies before evacuating. While Rommel's armies had suffered further heavy casualties during and since the retreat from the Mareth Line, the greater part of that which remained of the Afrika Korps, nevertheless, escaped northwards into the high ground to the north of Enfidaville. Since 20 March, when the attack on the Mareth Line opened, the Eighth Army alone had taken a further 20,000 prisoners in Tunisia. The pictures show: left, sappers of the Eighth Army repairing a bridge over the river at Gabes, which was blown up by the Germans as they retreated northwards; right, General Montgomery is seen entering the port of Sousse after its capture.

ports of Sfax and Sousse 10-12 April, 1943

CAPTURE OF FERRYVILLE

On 7 May, American forces entered Ferryville on the south shore of the Lake of Bizerta. Here is shown the great damage caused to the harbour by Allied air attack. On left of the jetty are the remains of an Italian 6,000-ton ammunition ship after a direct hit. After the explosion, parts of the ship were picked up miles away

ALLIED ARMIES CAPTURE TUNIS AND BIZERTA. At dawn on 6 May the British First Army, supported by masses of bombers and fighter bombers, launched the final offensive for Tunis from the south of the river Mejerda, east of Medjez-el-Bab. A few hours later our tanks, armoured cars and infantry had broken through the strongly fortified German positions at Massicault, sixteen miles from the city of Tunis. The British armoured columns then rolled on into the Tunisian plain, and on the afternoon of 7 May advanced elements of the First Army entered Tunis. They had covered about twenty-three miles in thirty-six hours despite stiff enemy resistance. Meanwhile, in the north the American and French troops, who began their offensive at precisely the same time as the First Army, were making equally rapid progress to Bizerta. An American force advancing northwards from Mateur cleared the enemy's stronghold on Jebel Achkel, on the south shore of Lake Achkel. After the capture of Ferryville, the Second U.S. Corps poured into Bizerta at 4 p.m. on 7 May. The pictures show: top, left, American tanks driving past smashed German guns; bottom, left, British patrol enters Tunis; above, American patrol enters Bizerta.

STREET FIGHTING IN TUNIS. Although the main body of the enemy had fled from Tunis by the time that British troops began to enter the city soon after midday on 7 May, many German snipers' nests had to be cleared up. German sappers were also blowing up munition dumps and installations. Consequently street fighting went on in the suburbs for many hours before all enemy resistance was liquidated. The pictures show: above, British Bren gunners in action in a Tunis street; below, a batch of German prisoners being marched away to internment.

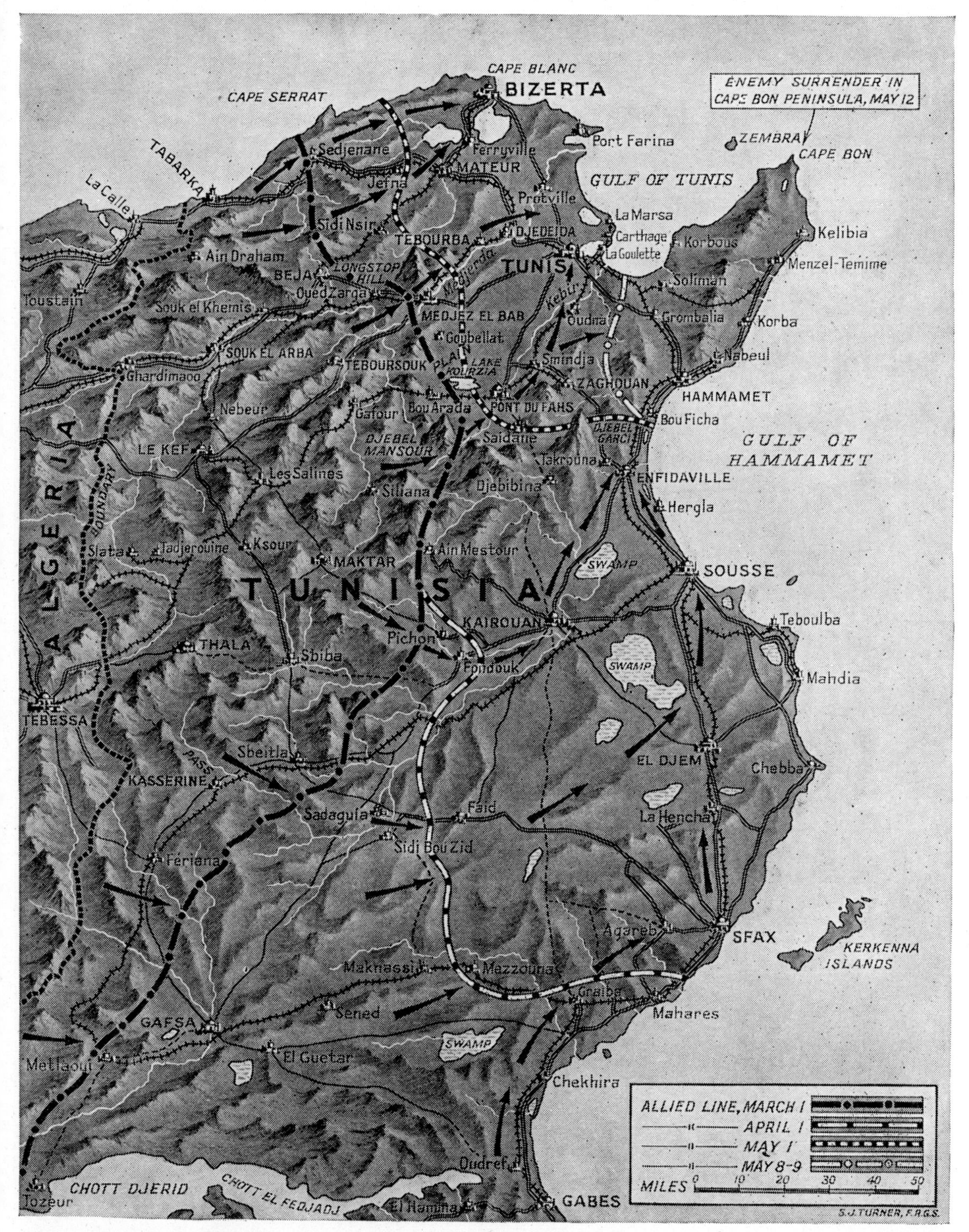

AXIS RETREAT IN TUNISIA. This map shows the stages of the Allied advance through Tunisia in the last two months of the campaign. Arrows indicate the main thrusts against the enemy: in the south by the Eighth Army, in the centre through the Kasserine Pass and Pichon by the First Army and Americans, and in the north the final British and U.S. drive on Tunis and Bizerta. The Axis forces were pushed back with increasing speed in April, and by 8-9 May their remnants were bottled up in Cape Bon peninsula, where they surrendered on 12 May.

ENEMY RETREAT TOWARDS CAPE BON. By the capture of Tunis and Bizerta the whole Axis defence system in the centre and northern parts of Tunisia was broken and their remaining forces cut into two. On the following day, 8 May, British armoured units made progress in a north-easterly direction from Tunis, linking up with American armoured units of the U.S. 2nd Corps advancing from Bizerta and Mateur. Farther south a force of Fighting French, operating with part of the British First Army, fought its way over many miles of difficult country and occupied the important town of Zaghouan. Meanwhile, in the most southerly sector, the Eighth Army, which had repulsed a small enemy attack north-west of Enfidaville on the previous day, made good progress and captured a large number of prisoners. Except at the entrances to the Cape Bon peninsula only a few isolated pockets of enemy resistance were left in Tunisia. The pictures on these pages, which were taken on the day before the fall of Tunis, show: top, left, British infantry take an enemy mortar position; bottom, left, a German killed beside his gun; above, British infantry approaching a ridge under fire from enemy mortars and artillery.

British Premier's s

CHURCHILL VISITS ROOSEVELT

It was officially announced on 11 May that the Prime Minister had arrived in Washington at the invitation of President Roosevelt. This was the fifth wartime meeting of the two Allied leaders. It took place earlier than had been expected because the sweeping Allied successes in North Africa—enemy resistance in the Cap Bon peninsula had collapsed and the surrender of the Axis forces remaining in Tunisia was imminent—necessitated conference and discussion upon the great problem of where Allied forces would make their next large-scale attack. A full review of the mighty problems o' armaments, supply, and transport for that attack was essential. Mr. Churchill's days in the American capital were taken up with meetings with political and service leaders and talks with President Roosevelt. Broadcasting to Britain from the White House, 14 May, on the occasion of the third anniversary of the Home Guard, Mr. Churchill :eft no doubt as to the purpose of the momentous conferences which were being held. "We are gathered here now, with the highest professional authorities in all the fighting services of the two great English-speaking nations, to plan well ahead of the armies who are moving swiftly forward. We must prepare for the time which is approaching and will surely come when the bulk of these armies will have advanced across the seas into deadly grapple on the Continent." On 19 May, in a speech to both Houses of the United States legislature, the Prime Minister declared: "Britain will wage war by America's side against Japan while there is breath in our bodies and while blood flows in our veins." He also gave Axis losses in Africa as 950,000 soldiers killed and captured, 2,400,000 gross tons o. shipping sunk, 8,000 aircraft destroyed, 6,200 guns, and 2,550 tanks lost. Mr. Churchill came home by air on 5 June. He had made the outward 'ourney by sea. The picture shows him leaving the battleship in which he had sailed.

WASHINGTON, 19 MAY, 1943
Historic session of the U.S. Congress addressed by British Prime Minister.

R.A.F. ATTACKS BIG GERMAN DAMS

On the night of 16-17 May a force of "Lancaster" bombers, led by Wing-Commander G. P. Gibson, D.S.O., D.F.C., carried out an attack with mines on the great Eder and Mohne dams in German Westphalia. The Mohne dam was breached over a length of 100 yards, the power station being swept away by the resulting floods. The destruction of the Eder dam—the largest in Europe—set the Eder river below it in full flood. Later R.A.F. reconnaissance pilots reported great havoc as 134,000,000 tons of water swept down the Ruhr valley, wrecking factories, power stations, villages, railways in their path. Eight "Lancaster" bombers were lost in the attacks, which were carried out from as low an altitude as 100 feet. Pictures show: .op, left, the breach left after the attack on the Eder dam; right, the breach in the Mohne dam; bottom, left, H.M. the King congratulating Wing-Commander Gibson after the raid.

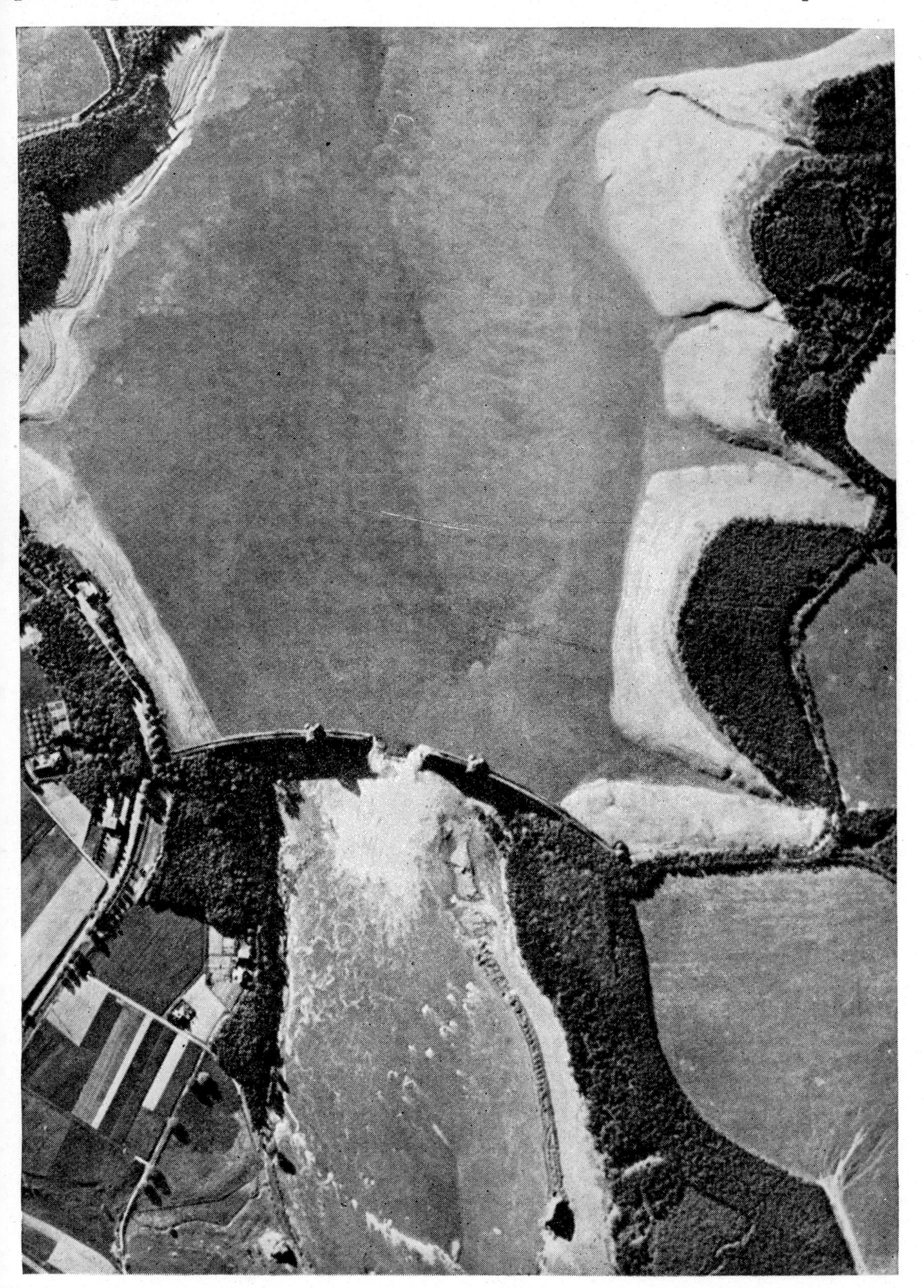

British aircraft haras

AIR ATTACKS ON THE ENEMY'S SEA ROUTES

Torpedo-carrying "Beaufighters" of Coastal Command successfully a tacked a German convoy off the Dutch coast on 17 May. The convoy, attacked from mast height, was evidently one of great importance, since it was protected by eight escorting vessels. The "Beaufighter" from which the picture, left, was taken was about to release a torpedo to attack vessel (1). "Beaufighter" (2) has already dropped torpedo (3) for its attack on ship (4). Waterborne balloons (5 and 6) are carried by the merchant vessels. At 7 and 8 bombs have been dropped by other attacking aircraft, and at 9 cannon-fire rakes the water where a vessel has taken evasive action. Lower pictures show: left, a "Beaufighter" flying away a moment after bombing an enemy ship; right, a doomed vessel after the attack.

RECOVERY OF ALEUTIAN ISLANDS CONTINUES. Following the earlier occupation of Adak Island (Andreanof Group), U.S. forces in January landed unopposed on Amchitka Island and consolidated their positions there. A further stage in the clearing of the Japanese out of the Aleutians was reached on 11 May when American forces had landed on Attu, the outermost of the islands, which is 650 nautical miles east of the nearest Japanese-owned base and 196 miles west of Kiska, the other Aleutian island seized by the enemy in June 1942. The Japanese had abandoned Attu the following September and reoccupied it in December. Under cover of a continuous bombardment from sea and air, the Americans poured a steady stream of reinforcements on to the island, and heavy fighting raged on the north coast around Holtz Bay. In spite of this the U.S. forces captured the high ground behind Holtz Bay, with what were reported to be slight casualties. On 18 May patrols from the American force advancing northwards from Massacre Bay joined up with the troops working inland from Holtz Bay. Later the same day the enemy withdrew to some high ground at the head of Chicagof harbour, where they attempted to make a stand,

but by 21 May American official announcements were able to declare that the fighting had developed into a mopping-up process and that the alternatives facing the Japanese were surrender or liquidation. In spite of sleet, snow and rain, which tended to handicap operations, the American pressure increased and was reinforced by heavy bombardments from the sea, which, added to the continuous air strafing, totally reduced all buildings in the Chicagof area by 26 May. At dawn on 29 May the Japanese launched a last desperate attack against the right wing of the U.S. forces in Chicagof valley and, with the exception of a few snipers, were completely annihilated. All organized enemy resistance thereupon collapsed. Two days later a broadcast from Washington said tha small remaining pockets of resistance on Attu were being mopped up, and fewer than 200 Japanese were fighting back from machine-gun nests. Of the garrison which Tokio announced to consist of just over 2,000 men, 1,845 were later reported to have been killed. Only twenty had been taken prisoner. The pictures show: left, part of the American landing force approaching Holtz Bay; and, right, men and equipment being put ashore at Massacre Bay.

BRITISH GUERRILLA EXPEDITION IN BURMA. On 20 May a guerrilla force of British, Indian and Australian troops led by Brigadier O. C. Wingate, D.S.O., returned to India after a three-months' wrecking expedition behind the Japanese lines in the jungle of Central Burma. These highly trained men had crossed the Assam-Burma frontier on 16 February, after which they operated in groups in the most difficult jungle and mountain country, penetrating more than 200 miles behind the enemy's lines. Frequently they went for many days without food or water and lived on whatever they could find till supplies could be dropped to them in the jungle clearings by parachute from British aircraft. They cut communication lines, destroyed bridges and supply dumps, and also killed hundreds of the enemy while suffering only light casualties themselves. The pictures show: left, supplies being dropped by parachute to the guerrillas in the jungle; and, above, Brigadier Wingate talking to the men under his command.

VICTORY CROWNS THE AFRICAN CAMPAIGN

By 12 May General Eisenhower was able to announce that organized resistance in all parts of Tunisia had ceased. He gave the highest praise to General Alexander for his strategy in the final offensive and for the manner in which he had deceived the enemy as to his intentions and accurately gauged how the enemy's mind would work. For 2,000 miles the Eighth Army had been the hammer and the First Army the anvil. Because of the efficiency and skill with which its long advance had been conducted, the Eighth Army had gained a well-deserved reputation as a fighting force, not only among the Allies, but in the minds of the enemy High Command as well. That the enemy's morale had snapped utterly was shown by a record which had been found of the German Commander-in-Chief's last signal. "I report," it read, "that the order to defend Tunisia to the last cartridge has been carr'ed out." The operator who handled the signal had given the lie to this, however, by adding below: "Everything destroyed; we are now closing down." The Germans, in fact, surrendered in mass, whole divisions capitulating with the.r arms, equipment and food. One dump alone, found undamaged, contained 12,000 tons of ammunition. In addition to General von Arnim, the supreme Axis commander captured by British troops, enemy prisoners totalled over 200,000, and vast quantities of abandoned enemy guns and war material fell into Allied hands. It was estimated that the enemy had suffered 30,000 casualties, killed and wounded. British casualties between 17 April and 7 May were 10,800 killed and wounded. In the final stages of the battle for Tunis, R.A.F. bombers flew 2,500 sorties in a day. Over an area of four miles by 1,000 yards scarcely a patch of surface escaped the rain of high explosives. In a message to General Eisenhower the King expressed the country's heartfelt congratulations on the Allied victory. In the Tunisian capital on 20 May units from all the Allied forces marched through the town in celebration of the victorious conclusion of the long African campaign. All the Allied commanders were present, and the salute was taken by Generals Eisenhower, Alexander, Anderson and Giraud. The picture on these pages shows the Tunis victory parade in progress headed by a band of pipers of the 51s Highland Division.

CHINA ON THE OFFENSIVE

At the close of six years' resistance to Japanese aggression, resourceful Chinese troops overcome all obstacles to surprise the enemy.

DEFENDING GATEWAY TO CHUNGKING. The Japanese attack early in May, south of the Yangtze River, failed. Two strongly reinforced Japanese divisions were routed with heavy losses and Chinese troops captured an important pass leading to Chungking. At the end of May the Chinese launched an offensive near the Hupeh-Honan border, trapping five enemy divisions. Above, Chinese troops move up to the front; top, left, long lines of Chinese reinforcements are on the march; and bottom, left, camouflaged Chinese soldiers in the firing line.

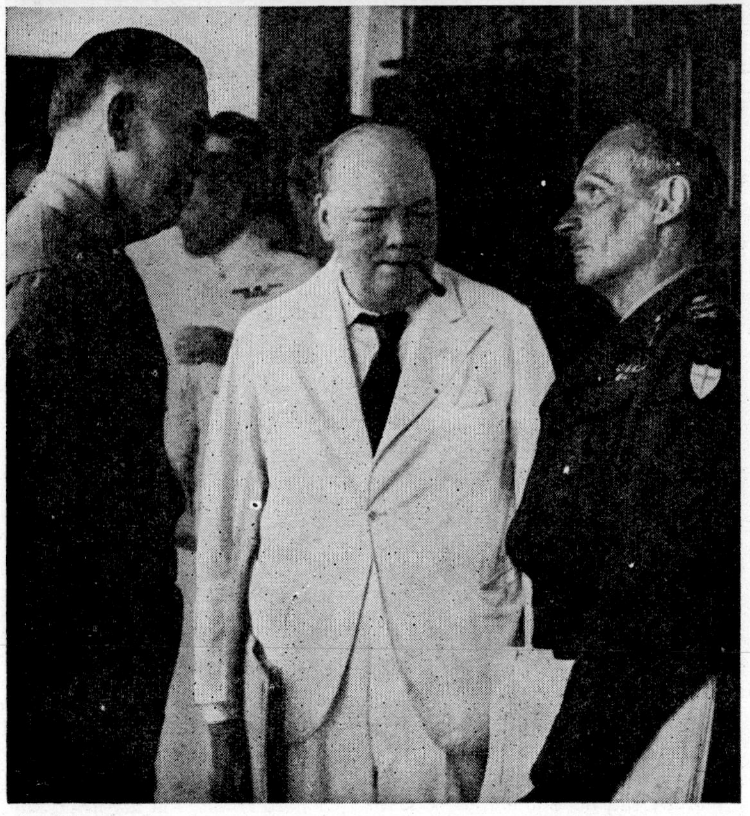

WAR CONFERENCE AT ALGIERS

On 27 May, after his visit to Washington, Mr. Churchill, accompanied by General Marshall (C.-in-C. U.S. Army) flew from the United States to Gibraltar. After spending one night there he proceeded to Allied Headquarters in North Africa and was joined in Algiers by Mr. Eden, who had flown from Britain. The Prime Minister had conversations with all the Allied leaders (among them Generals Eisenhower, Alexander, Anderson and Montgomery, Admiral Cunningham and Air Chief Marshal Tedder). He also met Generals Giraud and de Gaulle on 4 June. Mr. Churchill visited the Tunisian battlefields and addressed 3,000 British and American troops in the Roman amphitheatre in ancient Carthage, near Tunis (picture, right). The other pictures show: top, members of the War Conference; left, Mr. Churchill, General Montgomery and General Marshall in earnest conversation at Algiers.

DE GAULLE ARRIVES IN NORTH AFRICA. General de Gaulle, leader of the Fighting French since the fall of France in 1940, arrived in North Africa on 30 May for talks with General Giraud, Commander-in-Chief of the French forces in North Africa. This visit of General de Gaulle was the result of several months of negotiations between the French National Committee in London and General Giraud. The long-range exchange of views, effected through General Catroux, who had travelled to and from Britain with proposal and counter-

proposal, led eventually to General Giraud's agreement to a meeting at Algiers to discuss the co-ordination of Fighting French effort. Above, the two leaders of Free France are seen together. Their discussions culminated later in the establishment of the French Committee of National Liberation, presided over by the two Generals jointly. Meantime the French forces in North Africa, under General Giraud, were playing their part in the final Tunisian fighting. The picture on the left shows French troops unloading mules on the way to the Tunisian front.

ALLIES GAIN FOOTHOLD IN SOUTHERN EUROPE

After the Tunisian campaign came to an end and the Axis armies had been finally driven out of the African continent, the victorious Allies were soon in a position to make their next move in the Mediterranean war zone. The capture of the small, but strategically important, island of Pantelleria gave the British and U.S. air forces valuable advanced airfields to complement those of Malta and those along the North African shores. For any amphibious military operations against the Mediterranean coastline of Europe powerful support by fighter cover, or " air umbrella," was absolutely necessary. Indeed, as experience in this war had already shown, no landings on an enemy-occupied coast, however skilfully planned and boldly carried out, could hope to be successful without such fighter cover. The map on the right shows the approximate operational range of fighter aircraft based along the southern shores of the Mediterranean, including the islands of Malta and Pantelleria. It reveals quite clearly, therefore, why Sicily (although it was known to be the most strongly defended of all the chief Italian islands) was selected for the initial attack on the " under belly " of Europe, instead of Sardinia or Corsica. As the map shows, Sicily lay well within operational range of Allied fighter aircraft, whereas Sardinia was only partly within their range and Corsica was right outside it. It follows, therefore, that while fighters could have accompanied military landings on Sardinia, they could not have covered such landings in anything approaching sufficient strength. Over Sicily, on the other hand, strong fighter protection could be provided quite easily. Another important factor which the Allied commanders must have undoubtedly had in mind when the decision to attack Sicily was made was its possession of a large number of first-class airfields which would prove of the greatest value for the next step in the Mediterranean campaign, namely, the attack on the Italian mainland itself.

ROME
Velletri
Frosinone
Isernia
Campobasso
Foggia
Cassino
ITALY
ADRIATIC
SEA
GULF OF
MANFREDONIA
Barletta
Molfetta
BARI
Cerignola
Corato
GAETA
Benevento
Caserta
Monopoli
PONTINE
ISLANDS
Avellino
Spinazzola
Altamura
NAPLES
Vesuvius
BRINDISI
ISCHIA
SALERNO
Matera
Potenza
TARANTO
CAPRI
Lecce
GULF OF SALERNO
Metaponto
Otranto
ENIAN
EA
Lauria
GULF OF
TARANTO
GULF OF
POLICASTRO
Castrovillari
OXIMATE OPERATIONAL RANGE OF FIGHTER AIRCRAFT
Belvedere
Cariati
Paola
Cosenza
Amantea
Cotrone
Catanzaro
STROMBOLI
GULF OF
S. EUFEMIA
USTICA
GULF OF
SQUILLACE
Pizzo
LIPARI
ISLANDS
GULF OF GIOJA
Monasterace
Castellammare
Palmi
Milazzo
PALERMO
Scilla
Gerace
MESSINA
Cefalu
Reggio
STRAIT OF MESSINA
TRAPANI
Termini
Taormina
C. Spartivento
Melito
Marsala
Mt. Etna
Cape Corse
Nicosia
Giarre
Gulf of St. Florent
Castelvetrano
SICILY
Bastia
Sciacca
CATANIA
Caltanissetta
Calvi
Girgenti
Gerbini
Augusta
Corte
Cervione
Caltagirone
Gela
Syracuse
CORSICA
Licata
Comiso
Gulf of Sagone
Ragusa
Aleria
NEAN SEA
AJACCIO
Pachino
Cape Passero
Solenzara
Sartene
Strait of Bonifacio
GOZO
CAPRERA
ASINARA
VALETTA
Gulf of
Asinara
LINOSA
Terranova
MALTA
PIONE
SARDINIA
LAMPEDUSA

ALLIES CAPTURE PANTELLERIA. On 11 June the small Italian island of Pantelleria surrendered unconditionally. This immediately followed heavy day and night bombing and the shelling of enemy garrisons from the sea, after two previous Allied ultimatums, on 9 and 10 June, had been rejected. One hour after the surrender, troops of the British First Division began to disembark on the island. After having overcome some slight resistance put up by Italian snipers they quickly gained their objectives. The island was occupied at a very small cost in Allied casualties, though a force of German dive bombers made a last-minute attempt to prevent the landings by bombing landing craft. These attacks were quite ineffective, as all the bombs fell wide. The pictures show: left, "Baltimore" bombers over Pantelleria; top, right, shelling Pantelleria; bottom, right, the island in Allied hands.

THE KING IN NORTH AFRICA

On 12 June a Service plane with two wing commanders at the controls landed on a North African airfield. Luggage in the plane was labelled T. Jerram, but out stepped the King, to be welcomed by General Eisenhower, Admiral Cunningham, and Air Chief Marshal Tedder. He had borrowed the name of Guardsman Jerram, his batman, for his visit to the Eighth Army—the first time a King of England had ever flown to a battlefront. For several days he busied himself with consultations with service commanders, visits to the men of the forces, who welcomed him warmly, meetings with American military and naval leaders, and other activities. He spent a day with the Navy, shaking hands with many of the men who had seen action at Pantelleria, and talking to merchant sailors who had been engaged in hazardous convoy duty. With Sir Andrew Cunningham he visited units of the U.S. and British fleets in the Mediterranean, being piped aboard a British battleship and an American cruiser. The King inspected American infantry, watched a march past of armoured forces, and exercises in street fighting. He invited General Giraud and General de Gaulle to lunch, with Mr. Robert Murphy, the U.S. minister, and the British resident minister, Mr. Harold Macmillan. One of his visits, unofficial and unexpected, gave rise to a remarkable display of loyalty and enthusiasm. At a big convalescent rest centre by the sea, where several thousand soldiers were recuperating after wounds and illness, word flashed round that the King had arrived. Swiftly men raced to greet him, crowding, laughing, and cheering wildly, many of them dashing out of the water to be among the first to shake their visitor's hand. Suddenly somebody started the National Anthem. It was taken up with fervour and emotion, and when it had been finished the men cheered the King again and again. This picture shows the King walking between the packed lines of soldiers on the sands.

AIR BLITZ ON SICILY. Preparatory to invasion, the Allies flung their full air strength against Sicily, Sardinia, and the Italian mainland. In one period of twenty-four hours, concentrating upon Sicily, Allied bombers, strongly covered by fighters based on Malta, destroyed several hundred planes on Sicilian airfields and shot down forty-four enemy planes in the air for an Allied loss of thirteen. The airfields of Catania, Gerbini, Sciacca, Comiso, and Milo were all heavily attacked. Above, Martin "Marauders" of the U.S.A.A.F. bomb an Italian airfield.

CATANIA ATTACKED FROM THE AIR. Both before and during the invasion the large port and airfield of Catania were heavily bombed again and again, and enormous damage was done to the harbour and other important military targets. Though these raids often met with opposition, they provided significant evidence that the savage power of the Luftwaffe was weakening, for among the many types of Axis planes shot down, some were obsolete, and would not have been used but for shortage of aircraft. Above, huge fires in Catania after an Allied raid.

RENDOVA OCCUPIED. On 30 June U.S. Marines landed on Rendova, a mountainous island in the New Georgia group, 170 miles north-west of Guadalcanal. Enemy opposition was quickly overcome and within a few hours the whole island was occupied. Rendova is separated by only a seven-mile strait from New Georgia Island, where the Japanese held Munda and its important airfield. The picture above shows the Americans landing on Rendova. Those opposite: top, Australian troops at Sananda, New Guinea; and bottom, Japanese prisoners on Guadalcanal.

ALLIED INVASION OF SICILY

At 10 o'clock on Friday night, 9 July, gliders packed with Allied troops dropped behind the enemy lines in Sicily, and the invasion of the island had begun. The gliders were quickly followed by paratroops, and through the next two days American and British landing forces made contact with the airborne units, breached the coastal defences, and established bridgeheads at many selected points. Protected by a great fleet of Allied warships, and by the Allied Air Forces, which had secured air supremacy, mighty reinforcements of men, tanks, guns, equipment, and supplies were successfully landed. Enemy coastal batteries were put out of action by the guns of the Fleet. By 11 July the first immediate objectives had been taken, and three Sicilian airfields were in Allied hands. One of these was at Pachino, captured by British and Canadian assault troops. American forces occupied two airfields at Gela, where the enemy, supported by tanks, made a counter-attack, which was successfully beaten off. Axis forces opposing the invasion were estimated at 400,000, including 100,000 Italians. The German radio admitted that the first phase of the attack had been successful at several points, and an Italian commentator boasted that the Allies would "bite their teeth out" on the strong Italian fortifications. The picture shows one of the many Sicilian landings.

ZERO HOUR FOR INVASION ARMADA. Under the command of Admiral of the Fleet Sir Andrew Cunningham, 3,266 surface ships were engaged in the invasion of Sicily. This mighty armada of the Allies comprised craft of every type, from battleships to M.T.B.s. In spite of adverse changes in the weather, of rising wind and choppy seas, the convoys of this multitude of ships made their crossings with such precision that the Allied landings on the beaches were carried out exactly to timetable. From long before dawn flare after flare arose from beach after beach at the appointed zero hour to signal " landing successful," and thereafter all the supplies, arms, and equipment of the invading armies streamed steadily ashore. The Allied navies performed magnificently their arduous share of the invasion operations, inspired in their great task by the message which Admiral Cunningham sent to

every ship before embarkation: "Our primary duty is to place this vast expedition ashore in the minimum time and subsequently to maintain our military and air forces as they drive relentlessly forward into enemy territory. In the light of this duty great risks must be and are to be accepted." Before and during the landing, Admiral Cunningham's forces engaged enemy batteries and gun positions and warded off occasional attacks by fighter-bombers, while minesweepers worked to clear the heavily-mined anchorages. By 5 a.m. complete Allied air superiority had been obtained (zero hour for the landings along a 100-mile stretch of coastline was 3 a.m.). During these air operations twenty-two enemy aircraft were shot down by the R.A.F. over the Mediterranean and Sicily itself. Top, one of the landing beaches; bottom, left, Bren carrier comes ashore; bottom, right, scene at zero hour

ALLIED TROOPS STORM SICILY BEACHES. Glider-borne troops and paratroops formed the invasion spearhead in the great Allied attack on Sicily. They made their first landings before midnight on Friday, 9 July, their job being to seize special objectives and to capture the coastal defences from the rear. Before dawn on the next day seaborne troops swarmed from the landing craft, waded to the shore, and dashed up the beaches, defying

the pill-box defences and the guns of the enemy. Beach landings were successfully achieved along seventy miles of coastline, and by the night of Sunday, 11 July, British troops had taken Pachino, bridgeheads had been made good at many points, and 100 miles of the coast of Sicily was in Allied hands. Above is a vivid impression of the landing—the first large-scale landing along the western coasts of Europe—specially drawn by Forster.

FIRST WEEK OF SICILIAN INVASION

At dawn on Saturday, 10 July, the first assault troops landed on the Sicily beaches, and the success of the greatest amphibian operation in history was quickly proved. Before seven o'clock that morning all landings were established; Allied infantry were advancing into the interior; a few hours later the harbour of Syracuse was captured. British forces landed east of Cape Passero, Canadians on the western side, while United States forces came ashore at Gela. On the next day the Canadians took Pachino, and its airfield was very soon in use by Allied aircraft. On Tuesday, 13th, American forces captured Comiso and its airfield, joined up with the Canadians, and commanded the railway from Syracuse to Ragusa. By the next day seven of Sicily's airfields were firmly in the hands of the Allies. The Eighth Army successfully repelled fierce German counter-attacks. During Thursday and Friday the Eighth Army fought desperately for Lentini. The Americans and Canadians advanced and captured half a dozen towns. Lentini was occupied on Saturday, 17 July. Pictures show the amphibious DUKWS (known as " Ducks "), which were used with success in the landing operations. This six-wheeled lorry has a motor engine which drives wheels on land and a propeller at sea. Top, "Ducks" approaching shore; bottom, left, drawing away from a ship; right, returning for another load.

BRITISH AND CANADIANS JOIN HANDS. One of the early successes of the invasion was the determined capture of the Pachino peninsula by British and Canadian assault troops, who landed on Costa dell Ambra beach, four miles from Pachino. They established a bridgehead within twenty-four hours, and then advanced inland.

FIRST SICILY WOUNDED AWAIT EMBARKATION. Stretcher cases, wounded at Syracuse, waiting in landing craft to go aboard a hospital ship. On the first day of the invasion the hospital ship "Talamba," was deliberately bombed and sunk by the enemy, although the vessel was fully lighted in accordance with the Geneva convention.

EIGHTH ARMY'S THRUST FOR CATANIA. Within five days of the initial landings remarkable progress was achieved by the Allied forces. The U.S. Seventh Army under General Patton which had encountered strong enemy opposition, not only held firmly to the bridgeheads at Licata and Gela, but even enlarged them. New Allied landings were made near Catania, which was the goal of the famous Eighth Army under General Montgomery. Canadian units of his command joined up with the Americans at Ragusa, twenty miles inland, and Allied cruisers and monitors bombarded Augusta and entered the port on 13 July, a party from H.M.S. "Exmoor" hoisting the white ensign over the town. On 15 July the British advanced to Bruccoli, less than twenty miles from Catania.

Four Italian generals were killed in action, and another surrendered with all his staff. Seven airfields were securely in Allied possession, and prisoners taken in Sicily totalled 12,000. One of the airfields—Ponte Olivo—was taken by a fierce bayonet attack. German attempts to bring reinforcements into .he struggle were frustrated by heavy air attacks upon vital links of communication, Turin being heavily bombed by "Lancasters" which flew across France and returned by the Atlantic. Pictures show: top, left, troops of the 78th Division mopping up in a captured town; centre, enemy gun captured at Syracuse in firing order; right, Canadian miners at work; bottom, left, British infantry rounding up snipers near Augusta; right, civilians giving a welcome to British troops at Pachino.

THE CAMPAIGN IN SICILY

The Allied attack on Sicily began with massed airborne and naval landings in the south-east corner of the island on 10 July and virtually ended with the fall of Messina on 17 August. The island was finally occupied after only six weeks of hard fighting by British, Canadian and U.S. troops. They were delayed in their progress by the rugged and mountainous territory, by the difficulties of maintaining supplies and communications, and, not least, by the determined resistance of the German divisions, especially in the Plain of Catania. After the initial landings in the extreme south, the Allies soon gained their primary objectives, including many good airfields and the great port of Syracuse. Actually the enemy was taken completely by surprise, for, having expected the main Allied landings from the direction of Bizerta and other North-West African ports, they concentrated their main defences in the north-west corner of Sicily. What the Allies did, however, was to land a large part of their forces from Malta, where, on account of the shorter sea crossing, the landings could be made under the cover of massed fighter aircraft. After the main bridgeheads had been established along a coastline of roughly one hundred miles, the Allies fanned out as they proceeded to advance rapidly inland. The Americans drove westwards along the coast, captured Agrigento, and then advanced to Palermo, the occupation of which cut off thousands of Italian troops in the north-west corner. The Canadians captured Ragusa, then fought their way through to the centre of the island to take the important key towns of Enna and Leonforte. Meanwhile the Eighth Army advanced from Syracuse and Augusta towards the Catania Plain. It was here that the Germans made their greatest stand. The Eighth Army's break-through towards Randazzo and Messina was thus delayed until U.S. and Canadian troops were able to sweep down from the north coast and smash the German rear.

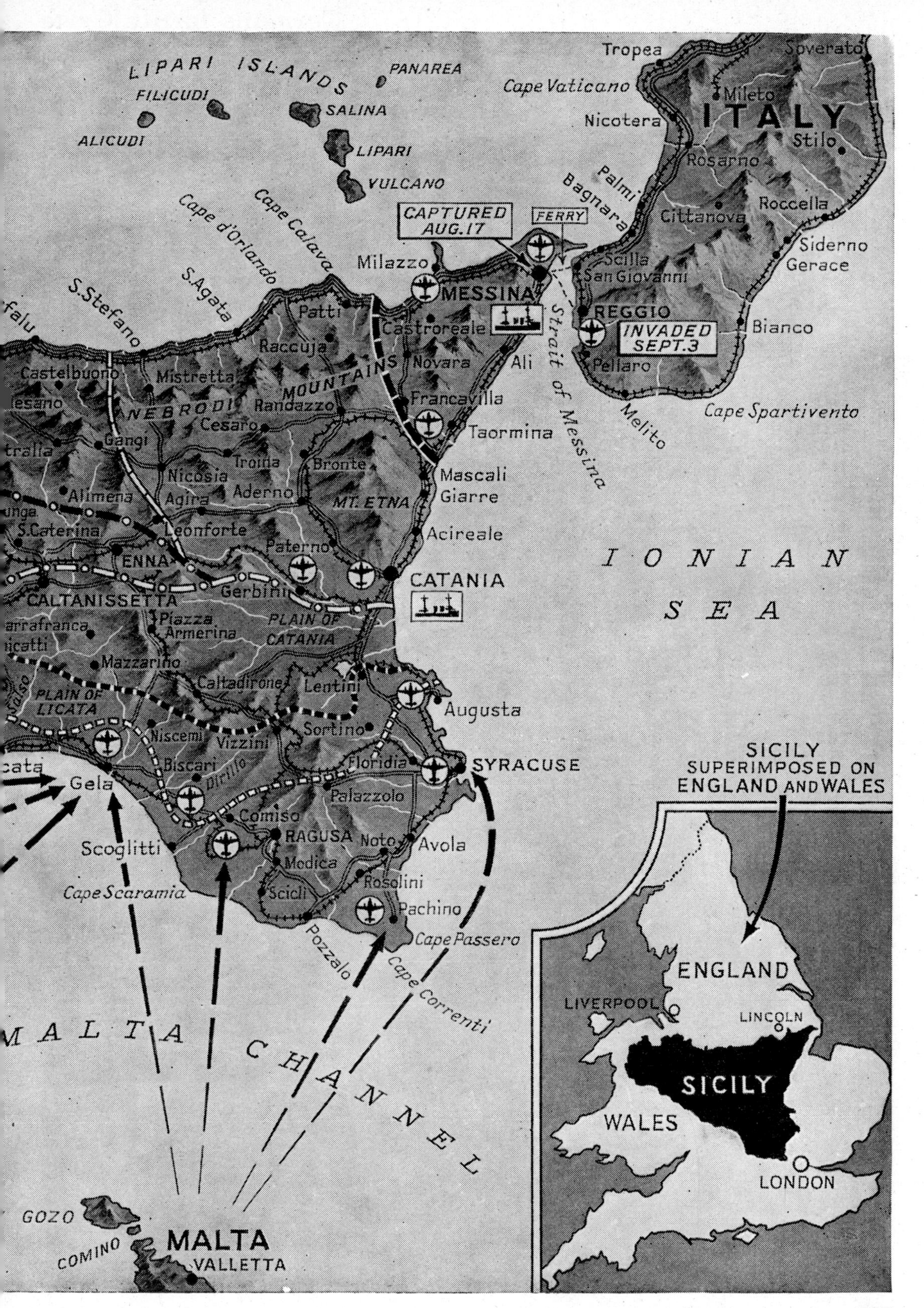
LIPARI ISLANDS
PANAREA
FILICUDI
SALINA
ALICUDI
LIPARI
VULCANO
Cape d'Orlando
Cape Calava
S.Agata
S.Stefano
CAPTURED AUG.17
FERRY
Milazzo
MESSINA
Patti
Castroreale
Raccuja
Novara
Castelbuono
Mistretta
MOUNTAINS
NEBRODI
Randazzo
Francavilla
Cesaro
Gangi
Taormina
Troina
Bronte
Nicosia
Mascali
Giarre
Alimena
Aderno
Agira
MT. ETNA
S.Caterina
Leonforte
Acireale
Paterno
ENNA
CATANIA
CALTANISSETTA
Gerbini
Piazza Armerina
PLAIN OF CATANIA
Mazzarino
Caltagirone
Lentini
PLAIN OF LICATA
Augusta
Sortino
Niscemi
Vizzini
Floridia
SYRACUSE
Biscari
Gela
Palazzolo
Comiso
RAGUSA
Noto
Avola
Scoglitti
Modica
Rosolini
Cape Scaramia
Scicli
Pachino
Cape Passero
Pozzalo
Cape Correnti
MALTA CHANNEL
GOZO
COMINO
MALTA
VALLETTA
Tropea
Soverato
Cape Vaticano
Mileto
Nicotera
ITALY
Stilo
Rosarno
Palmi
Bagnara
Cittanova
Roccella
Siderno
Gerace
Scilla
San Giovanni
REGGIO
INVADED SEPT.3
Bianco
Strait of Messina
Ali
Pellaro
Melito
Cape Spartivento
IONIAN SEA
SICILY SUPERIMPOSED ON ENGLAND AND WALES
ENGLAND
LIVERPOOL
LINCOLN
SICILY
WALES
LONDON

GERMAN FEARS OF INVASION. The Allied victories in North Africa represented, in the words of the Prime Minister, an immediate threat to the "soft under-belly of Europe" and the occupying German and Italian forces on the island of Crete reacted in characteristic fashion to the danger. A British commando raid on airfields and installations in Crete on the night of 3-4 July was followed by savage reprisals against the civilian population, accused by the Nazis of connivance in the raid. The picture, top, left, gives some idea of the cold-bloodedness in which these barbarous atrocities were committed. The other pictures show strong Nazi-built fortifications in Crete, the construction of which was greatly hastened after a special visit of inspection made by von Kesselring.

FRESH GERMAN ATTACK IN RUSSIA FAILS. On 5 July an intensive enemy artillery and aerial bombardment broke the comparative lull which had continued on the Russian front since the spring thaws had brought large-scale operations to a standstill. Large German tank and infantry forces with strong air cover launched the expected enemy summer offensive on a 200-mile front in the Orel-Kursk-Byelgorod sector. The battle that ensued developed into some of the bitterest fighting of the war, with both sides throwing in masses of armour and

infantry. But in spite of minor breaches of their positions here and there, made at enormous cost to the enemy, the Russians, by their stubborn resistance, completely neutralized the German attempt to repeat their massed drive to the East in the previous summer. By 14 July the enemy attacks had dwindled and, indeed, the Germans had again been forced back to their original positions. The photograph shows Red Army troops attacking an enemy strong point in a Russian village near Orel. Note the hooded uniform worn by the soldiers for camouflage

RUSSIAN SUMMER OFFENSIVE BEGINS. On 12 July, after the failure of the recent German assault on their positions, the Red Army launched a powerful offensive on a twenty-five-mile front to the north and east of Orel. Within three days the enemy's fortifications had been pierced to a depth of twenty-eight miles and three German infantry divisions and two Panzer divisions utterly routed. On 17 July the Red Army began their mighty attack on the Orel-Kursk-Byelgorod sector, and it was soon apparent that, not only had the German plan of a summer offensive, as Marshal Stalin announced, been " completely frustrated," but, in fact, the Russians had achieved a victory of the first magnitude. The Red Army eliminated all the wedges that had been driven into their positions in the abortive German offensive. The pictures on these pages show : above, Red Army tanks taking up their fighting stations before the Russian offensive began; top, right, German infantry in retreat use every kind of transport to escape encirclement or annihilation; bottom, right, German soldiers firing a Russian village as they retreat.

FIERCE FIGHTING BEFORE OREL. During the remainder of July fighting continued on a big scale in the Orel sector. Despite heavy rains and strong German resistance the Red Army advanced steadily, and by 1 August they had reached places within twelve miles o. the city. The pictures on these pages show Red Army cavalry in action. The Cossacks, especially, played a great part in the Don and Caucasus fighting earlier in the year. Left, Cossack warriors on horseback going into battle; above, Red Army cavalry crossing a river.

RUSSIANS WIN GREAT DOUBLE VICTORY. On 5 August Moscow radio announced the recapture of Orel and Byelgorod exactly one month after the Germans began their unsuccessful offensive on this front. Orel, which had been in German hands for nearly two years, was one of the chief enemy bases in Russia during that time. While the fighting for Orel and Byelgorod lasted, the Red Army inflicted very severe losses on their enemy, losses that would surely have serious repercussions on morale in the German forces. Between 5 July

and 5 August the German losses were 100,000 killed and 4,600 tanks, 1,623 guns, 11,000 lorries, and 2,500 aircraft, while in the same period the Red Army captured 521 tanks, 875 guns, 2,521 machine guns, 325 supply dumps and 12,400 prisoners. Yet on the eve of the offensive Hitler himself had issued an order of the day, declaring that that attack would be "the turning-point of the war and the last battle for Germany's victory." Picture shows a Russian collective farmer returning to her homestead laid waste in ruins by the hated Nazi invaders.

ARCHITECT OF FASCISM OVERTHROWN

As the Allied forces pressed north in Sicily and came within sight of the Italian mainland, Mussolini, first Fascist dictator, found himself facing internal revolt, which increasingly revealed itself in strikes and sabotage. So serious was the situation on both the war and the home fronts that he went to consult Hitler, who met him at Verona on 19 July. Hitler's proposed remedies were reported by Mussolini to the Fascist Grand Council, specially summoned to Rome on 24 July. But the writing was already on the wall for this "sawdust Cæsar"; a majority of the Council rejected his proposals, and the cornered and frantic Duce was forced to resign. To the people of Italy the tidings came like the sweet breath of Freedom, unsavoured for twenty-one weary years, and in the cities and towns the jubilant crowds demonstrated in the streets for days. To all outside Italy, particularly the millions suffering under Nazi oppression, the fall of Mussolini brought new confidence that his imitator across the Alps would meet the same fate. Pictures on this page show: top, what the citizens of a Sicilian town did to one of his innumerable effigies; below, the effacing of one of the slogans he had caused to be painted on public buildings all over Italy. This one reads: "Great Britain has finally felt deeply the bite of the Roman wolf." On the opposite page an Italian crowd is shown hurling over-ripe fruit at another of Mussolini's portraits.

DUCE

AMERICAN AIRCRAFT SHATTER RUMANIAN OILFIELDS. Ploesti and its famous oilfields, covering an area of nineteen square miles, were bombed for the fourth time on 1 August. Nearly 200 "Liberators" and 2,000 specially-trained airmen took part in this very heavy attack on a target of vital importance to the enemy—it was estimated that Ploesti, thirty-five miles from Bucharest, supplied one-third of all the oil fuel Germany required for war purposes. This mass raid involved a round journey of 2,400 miles. It was carried out at low level, many of the aircraft attacking from 500 feet and under, to ensure accurate placing of their bombs. They smashed down 270 tons of high-explosives upon the thirteen oil refineries, the pumping stations, and the storage tanks, causing huge explosions and devastating damage. Many of the installations were put out of action. Much of the destruction was done by delayed-action bombs. Above, one of the attacking aircraft sweeps in just over the smoke-stacks, against a background of smoke and flame. Top, right: "Liberators" streaking into the attack through a gap in the dense smoke clouds; below, one of the storage tanks going up in flames during the first moments of the raid.

EIGHTH ARMY IN AUGUSTA. Troops of the Eighth Army occupied the Italian naval and seaplane base of Augusta after it had been repeatedly bombed by the R.A.F. and shelled by the Royal Navy. The first ship to enter the harbour was the Greek destroyer "Kanaris," which engaged the shore batteries as she steamed in. Not only during the landings, but throughout the course of the Sicilian expedition, the Allied navies played a great part in supporting the land forces, subjecting Sicily to fifty organized bombardments. Above, British troops in Augusta.

CAPTURE OF CATANIA. Early on 5 August troops of the Eighth Army entered Catania. The people of the city welcomed the men of the victorious army with extraordinary enthusiasm. They clapped and shouted: "Viva!", they seized the soldiers' hands to shake them, they danced down the bomb-shattered streets by the side of the marching men. And they begged for food. The fall of Centuripe, a mountain stronghold with ridge on ridge held by German snipers, which the 78th Division had gallantly captured after savage fighting, had made the fall of Catania certain. Above: British troops passing through one of the many bomb-stricken streets in Catania.

Looting in Catani

RIOTS BEFORE THE ALLIES TAKE CATANIA

General Montgomery's personal message to the troops on 1 August made it clear that a new Allied offensive in Sicily had begun. "Let us get on with the job," said General Montgomery. "Together with our American Allies, we knocked Mussolini off his perch. We will now drive the Germans from Sicily. Into battle with stout hearts. Good luck to you all." After brilliant successes in the opening stages of the Sicilian campaign, the advance of the Eighth Army had been halted by the enemy's formidable line of defences along the Simeto river. The strongest bastions of that line were at Regalbuto and Centuripe. After much hard fighting the Eighth Army succeeded in occupying the mountains dominating the Simeto valley. The Canadians occupied Regalbuto, and the Americans captured Troina and Capizzi. The Prime Minister promptly informed the House of Commons of their successes: "Our general offensive in Sicily began to develop on Sunday afternoon (1 August), and all Monday was passed in full battle. Large reinforcements have been moved up to the fighting front, and it has been properly garnished with artillery and supplies of every kind." The 78th Division won a notable victory by storming the fortress-like position of Centuripe. The success compelled the Germans to begin the evacuation of Catania, enabling Allied forces to enter the Catanian plain. On 5 August Catania surrendered to the British Army. Picture shows Italians looting buildings in Catania which had been occupied by the Germans.

SICILY CONQUERED

After the fall of Catania on 5 August, British and Canadian forces pressed forward and made important gains north of Regalbuto. The Eighth Army pressed northward along the coast road to Messina, fifty miles away. Ships of the British Navy kept up a heavy bombardment of Messina. The Germans made every effort to delay the advance of the Allies by mines and large scale demolitions, but numbers of Germans and Italians were already assembling on the beaches of Messina preparatory to evacuation, and evacuation barges were being pounded and sunk by Allied planes. The Allies remained masters of the air. According to R.A.F. calculations, 12,000 German and Italian aircraft had been destroyed in the Middle East and North African campaigns since the entrance of Italy into the war. In Sicily alone, up to the surrender of Catania, the number of Axis prisoners was 100,000. On 10 August the Eighth Army and the U.S. Seventh Army linked up between Troina and Randazzo, and on the 17th the honour of capturing Messina fell to the Americans. All organized resistance on the island ceased. After a campaign of thirty-nine days the Sicilian campaign was over. Up to 10 August Axis losses were 167,000—32,000 killed or wounded and 135,000 prisoners. Allied casualties were 25,000 killed, wounded, and taken prisoner. Axis losses in tanks were 260 against 103 Allied tanks lost. Picture: Highlanders use captured German mules over the mountains beyond Catania.

FALL OF TAORMINA. On 16 August Eighth Army troops captured Taormina. The Germans fought stubbornly in rearguard actions, but enemy evacuation was steadily going on. Enemy troops were escaping over the Straits of Messina, at the rate of a thousand a day, while the R.A.F. kept up an almost ceaseless attack on the beaches, and on the ferries, barges, and lighters crammed with beaten fugitives. Messina, which had been the target o.

many attacks by the R.A.F. and the U.S.A.A.F., was again heavily bombed. Pictures: top, the "Bishop" self-propelled gun-tank combination, which did much effective work in the mountainous Sicilian country; bottom, left, British patrol passing the dead bodies of Italians in a street of Avola, which was captured by the Allied armies on the same day as Taormina; right, wrecked German troop-carrying tractor in bomb crater on Messina waterfront.

YUGOSLAV GUERRILLAS HARRY THE ENEMY. Patriot forces opposing the enemy occupying armies in Yugoslavia intensified their resistance over still wider objectives, and the Yugoslav Government G.H.Q. in Cairo reported on 28 August a number of recent successes. These included a daring attack on the Rajlovac (Serajevo) airfield on 10 August and the consequent destruction of twenty-eight German aircraft; the ambushing of a German armoured train near Serajevo: the capture of three towns, including an important coal-mining centre, in Bosnia and Slovenia; also the cutting at numerous places of the railway line in Dalmatia and the wrecking of key bridges. Some idea of the heroism behind the blows which the partisans were striking came from the enemy in this series of pictures showing: above, a lamp-post hanging of a patriot by the Germans in Belgrade; top, right, guerrillas captured by German troops; and, below, a band of captured guerrillas being marched to execution.

MAMMOTH HARVEST
Biggest crops in Britain's history were safely gathered in time by U.S. Army volunteers and by workers on holiday.

Nazis force peasants t

NAZIS STEAL UKRAINE HARVEST. German spokesmen declared on more than one occasion that the German people would not go short of food, whatever might be the plight of the inhabitants in the countries Germany had overrun. The Nazis carried out systematic and ruthless pillage of the resources of the occupied countries. They forced whole populations of Russian villages into slave labour, compelling them to help gather the harvests of the Ukraine, and sending the full yield to Germany. Vast agricultural tracts in the rich Ukraine passed into their

possession. When the brilliant successes of the Red Army in the summer campaign of 1943 forced the Germans to retreat, the latter made every effort to secure the harvest for their own use. It is estimated that they obtained from the Ukraine nearly half a million tons of grain for the needs of their invading armies. They deported numbers of the Russian population to Germany. Top, Nazi guns on fields during harvest; bottom, left, Russians forced to work under German guard; right, Nazi soldiers speed up the harvest and dispatch the crop home to Germany.

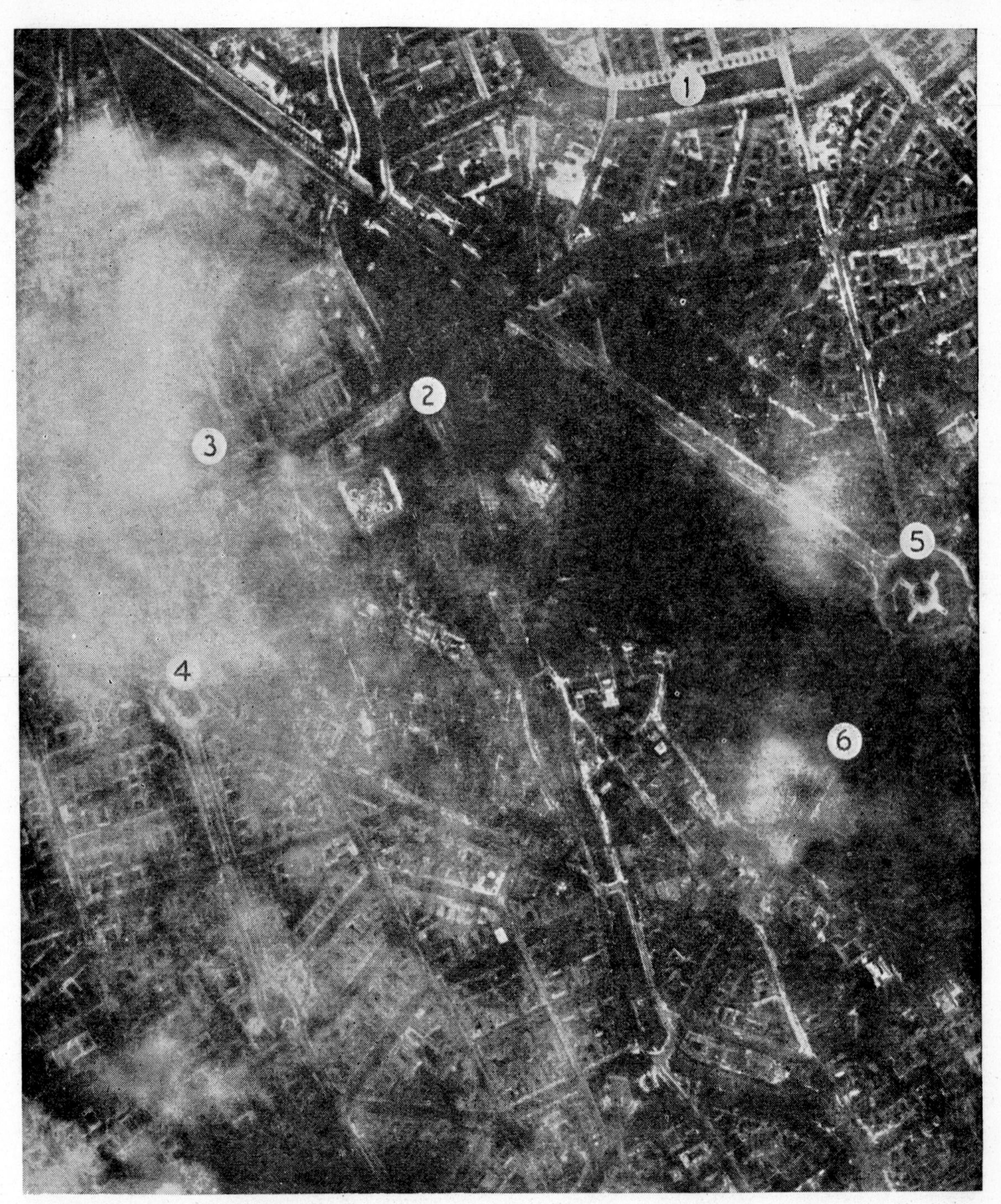

SMASHING AIR ATTACK ON BERLIN. Bomber Command of the R.A.F. smashed Berlin on 23 August in the heaviest and most concentrated attack the capital of Germany had ever experienced. Seven hundred planes took part. In fifty minutes they dropped 1,700 tons of bombs, causing enormous devastation. Great fires were still burning at the end of the next day, and reconnaissance aircraft reported vast clouds of smoke four miles high. Important electrical works and plants were badly damaged, and railway stations were wrecked. Above, a reconnaissance photograph which reveals one hundred fires still burning and shows distinctive features of the city: 1, River Spree; 2, two "flak" towers, on which A.A. guns are mounted; 3, Zoo station; 4, Augusta Victoria Platz; 5, Grosse Stern; 6, Tiergarten. Top, right, women leaving the city; below, women sleeping out.

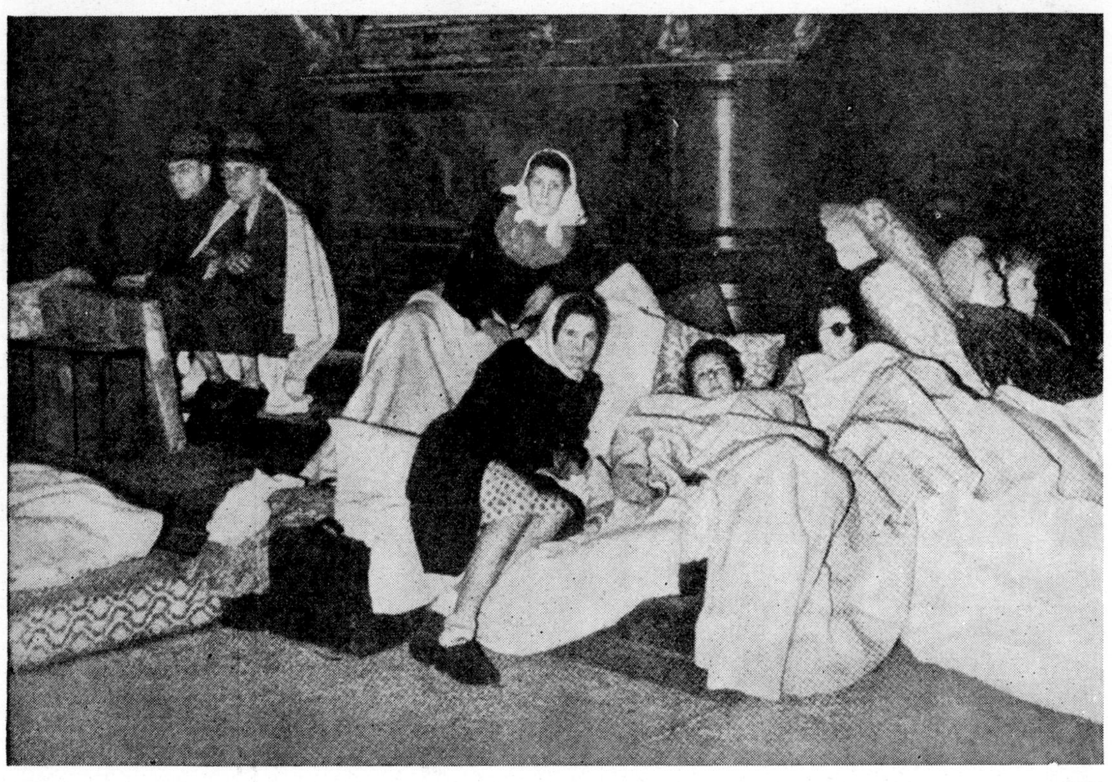

THE BATTLE OF BERLIN. In just over a week after the big attack with 1,700 tons of bombs, a great 'orce of R.A.F. bombers carried out on 31 August another devastating onslaught on Berlin. This time the attack ıasted forty-five minutes, and 1,000 tons of high-explosive and incendiary bombs were dropped. Forty-seven British planes were lost. Numbers of the German night fighters were shot down by the bombers. Pictures show

scenes in the city and outskirts on the days following the raid by the R.A.F.; left, Berliners having a meal in the open air, with a large burned-out building in the background; top, right, bombed-out people living in the woods outside the city, where light wooden shacks were hurriedly put together to shelter citizens whose houses had been destroyed; bottom, right, men and women receiving food from an emergency kitchen set up in Berlin.

NEW SUCCESSES BY RED ARMY. The Russians followed up their success at Orel and Byelgorod with a six-mile advance on 6 August, when they reoccupied over seventy inhabited places. On both the Bryansk and Kharkov fronts the Germans were driven back in hopeless disorder as the Russian advances gained momentum. On 12 August, after defeating strong enemy counter-attacks, the Red Army recaptured Chuguyev, an important German base twenty miles south-east of Kharkov, and two days later bitter street fighting was raging in the northern suburbs of the city. The victory at Chuguyev was swiftly succeeded by fresh advances

on the Bryansk front, where the Russians liberated yet another sixty localities including the towns of Aktinino and Novlya, a junction of the Bryansk-Kharkov and the Bryansk-Konotop railways. For several days the enemy launched one counter-attack after another, throwing in huge tank and infantry forces, and although their fury temporarily held up the Red Army they were all repulsed. With losses estimated at 4,000 men a day the Germans began to show signs of exhaustion. Meanwhile, of course, they were subjected to heavy day and night blows by the Red Air Force. The picture on these pages shows some Russian infantrymen driving the enemy from a village.

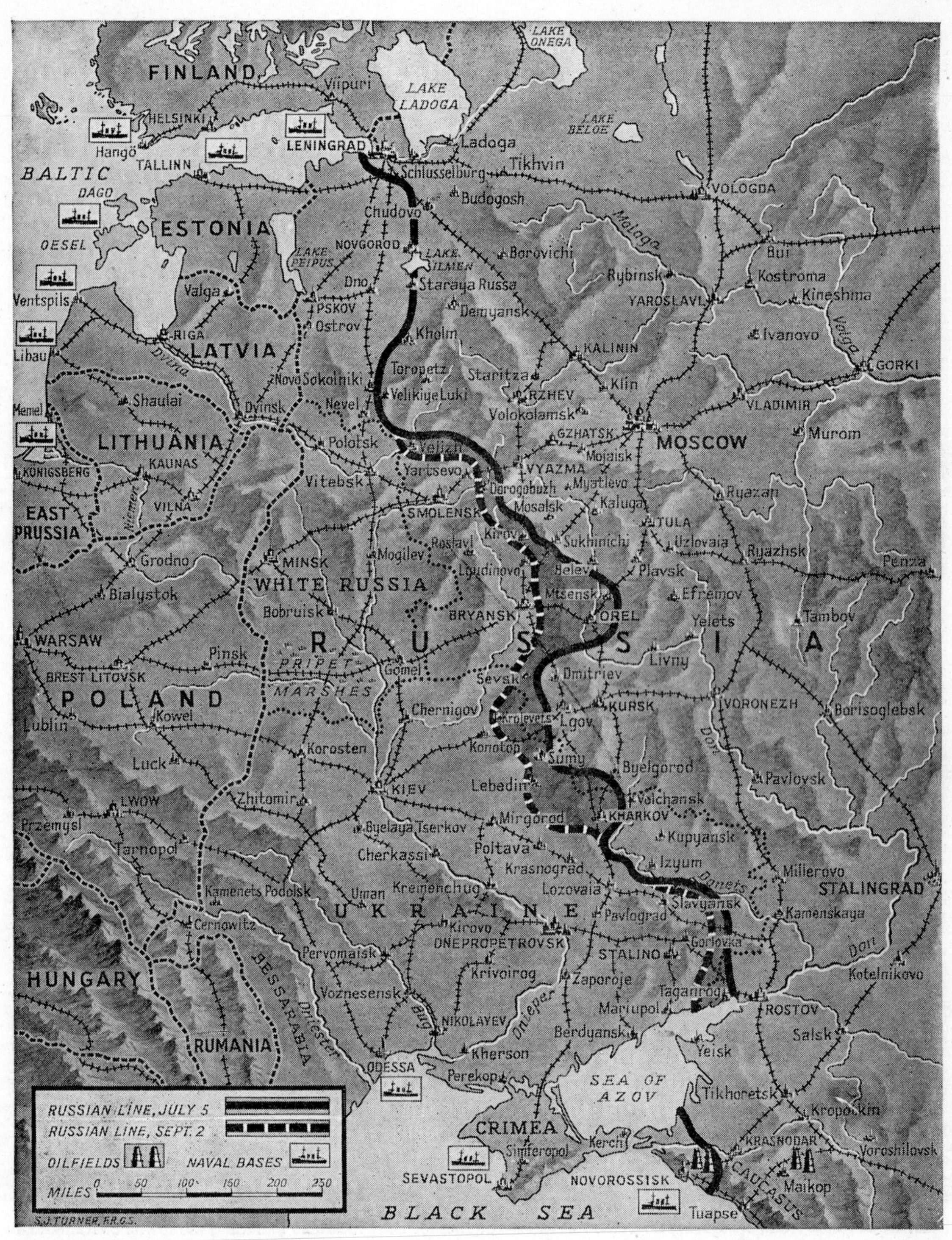

RED ARMY RECAPTURES KHARKOV. During the course of the war between Russia and Germany, Kharkov, the second largest city of the Soviet Union, had been four times captured. Twice the inhabitants of the city had known the bitterness of subjection to the German invaders. After retaking Rostov in February, the Red Army had delivered Kkarkov. But they had been unable to hold the city. On 15 March the Germans again entered Kharkov, and made it one of the most important bastions of the summer campaign. They strove hard to keep

the city, but despite all their efforts the Russians attacked desperately time and again, pressing their attacks on three sides with such success that eventually they had all but ringed the city, leaving the enemy the use of only one railway. Thus they forced the Germans to evacuate Kharkov and to retreat, narrowing the enemy's escape corridor to twenty miles in some places, and on 23 August Kharkov was liberated again. The map, left, shows limit of Russian summer advance. Top, right, Germans retreat from Orel; below, a bridge blown up by the enemy.

GERMANS RETREAT ALONG WHOLE RUSSIAN FRONT. During the last days of August the Red Army improved its positions along a vast front from the Smolensk area to the Sea of Azov. Progress was especially good on the Kharkov front where, on 27 August, the Russians reoccupied Kotelva, sixty miles west of Kharkov. Meanwhile, our victorious Allies pressed on to Taganrog, the important Sea of Azov port, which they recaptured on 30 August. Pictures show: left, a German outside a blazing farmstead; above, a Russian family returns home.

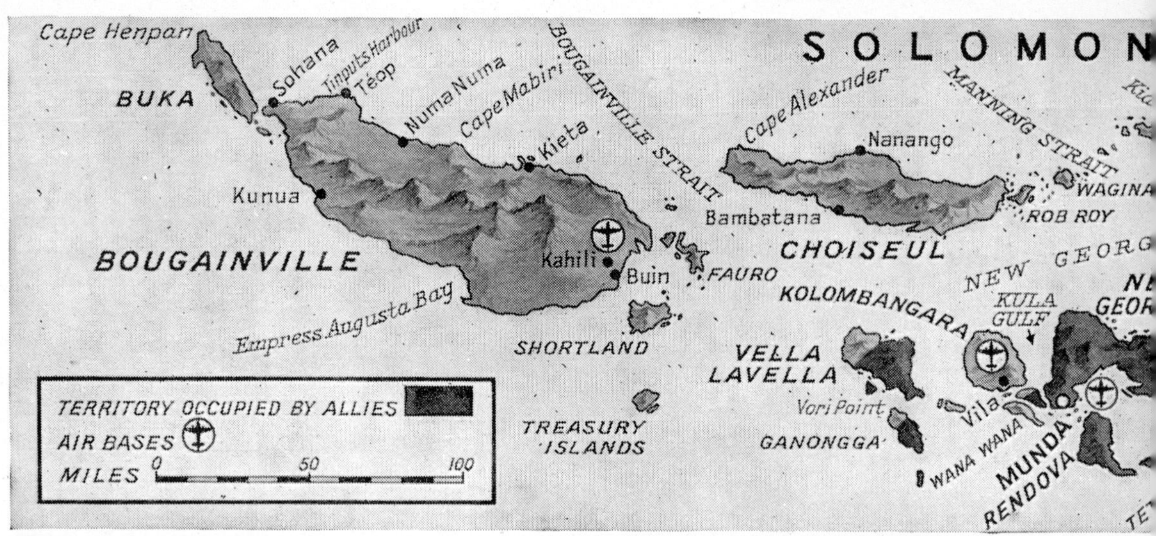

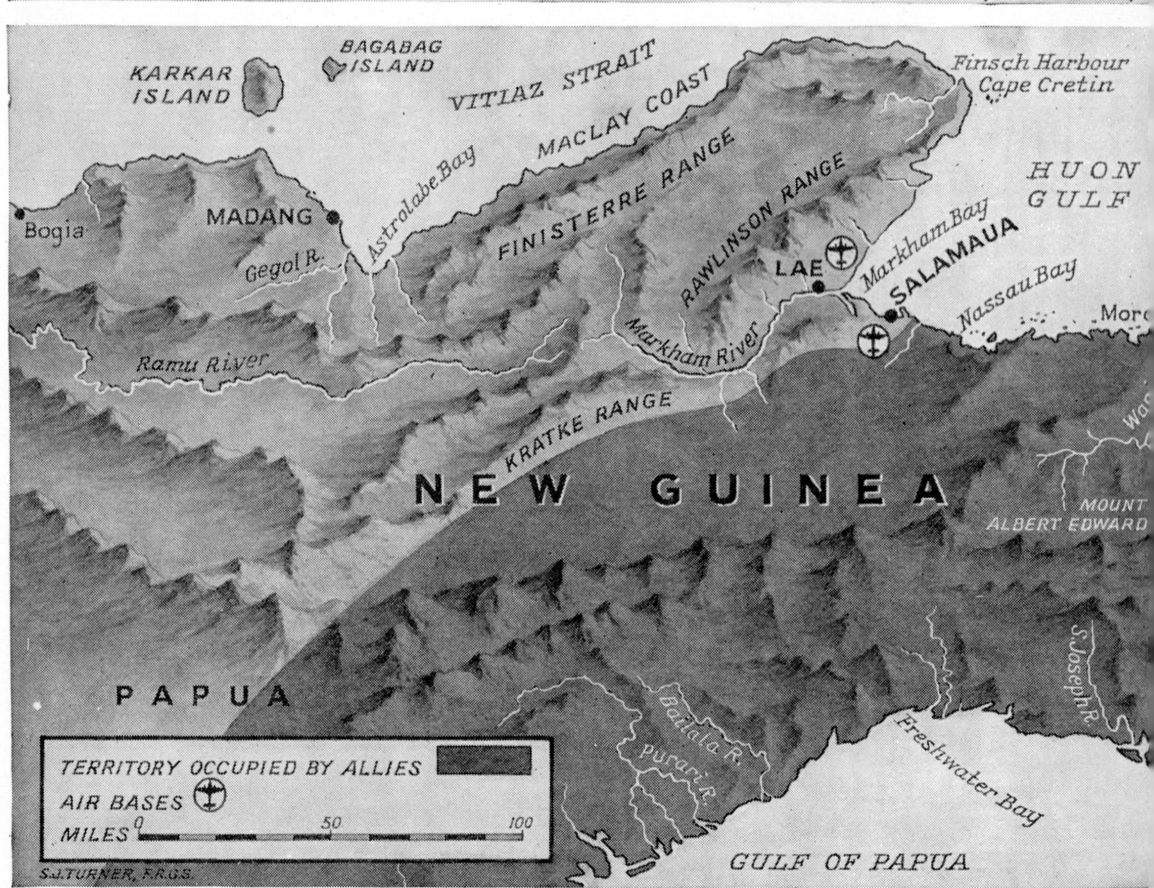

ALLIED VICTORIES IN SOUTH-WEST PACIFIC. The Allied campaign in New Guinea and the Solomons during 1942-1943 tied down large Japanese forces and also harassed the enemy's far-stretched lines of communications, while the main effort of the United Nations was directed to defeating Germany in the West. Considering the appalling conditions experienced by our fighting troops, great success was achieved. Moreover, heavy and increasing strain was put on Japanese sea communications since Allied sea and air power in the Pacific took great toll of all enemy shipping bringing up reinforcements and supplies. The maps on

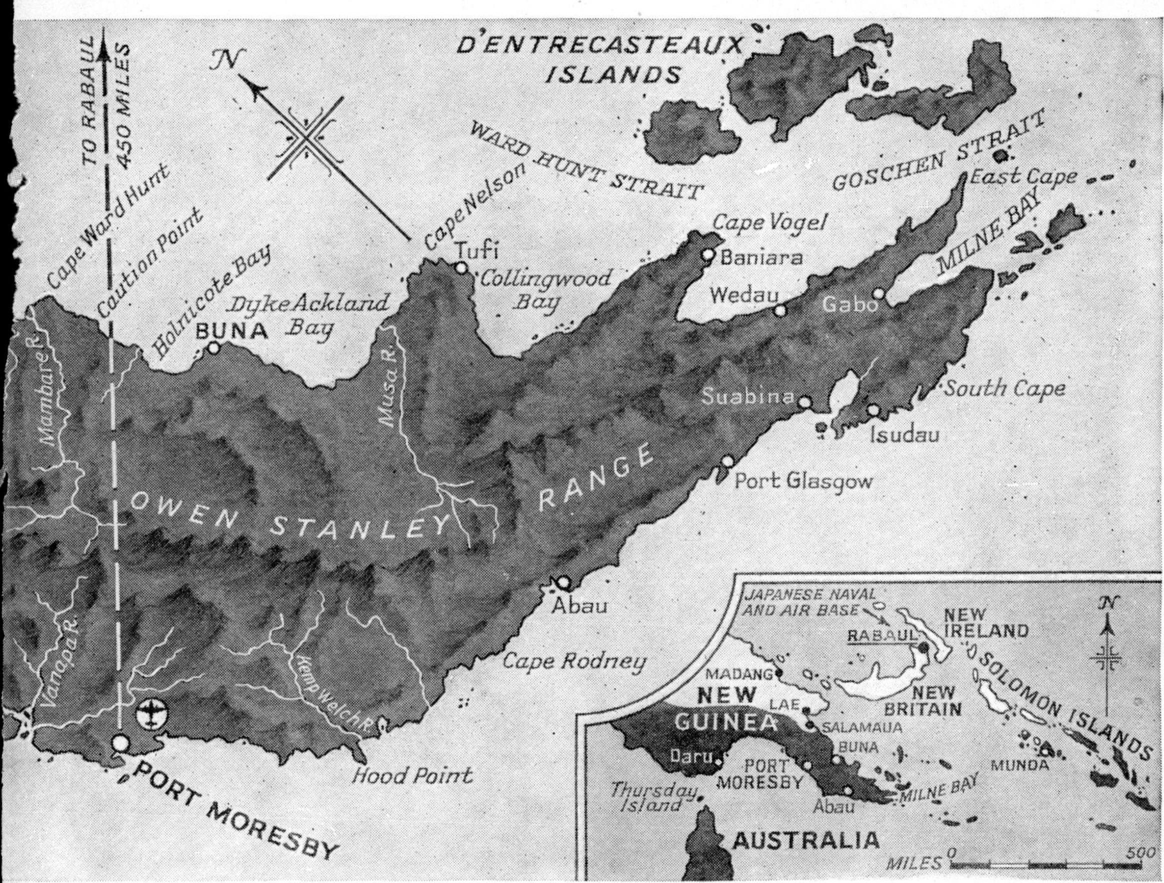

these pages show the Allied position in the South-West Pacific area by 1 September. The Papuan area of New Guinea, lower map, had been freed of the enemy, thereby relieving the immediate threat to Australia, and the Allies were advancing on Salamaua. Having completed the reconquest of Guadalcanal early in 1943, U.S. forces landed on Rendova and New Georgia, both of which were occupied by August. The upper map shows the course of the Allied drive westwards in the Solomons. By the creation of a South-East Asia Command under Lord Louis Mountbatten on 25 August, further operations against the Japanese in this area were to be expected.

ALLIES ADVANCE IN THE PACIFIC. After landings which began on 15 August, the island of Kiska in the North Pacific was retaken by United States and Canadian forces. The loss of Attu by the Japanese had jeopardized the enemy's supply lines and rendered enemy positions on Kiska hazardous, and Japanese troops evacuated the island under cover of fog. Far south, in the South-West Pacific, the Allies made good progress in New Guinea, employing their superiority in the air to smash the important airfields of Lae so thoroughly that

the Japanese were unable to make use of them for any effective retaliation. This terrific " softening " of Lae was carried out systematically by U.S. heavy bombers, "Liberators" and "Fortresses," in preparation for invasion. The Allies were determined to secure the great advantages wh'ch possession of the harbour and airfields of Lae would give them. Left, bombs bursting on a Jap airfield at Lae; right, top, United States troops land on Kiska Island; below, two midget submarines wrecked and abandoned by the Japanese before their retreat from Kiska.

FORTRESS WALL OF EUROPE. The German nation had become very apprehensive about Allied invasion, and leading German speakers boasted that their fortifications and coast defences on the coasts of the Atlantic and the Mediterranean were impregnable. Parties of Press correspondents were conducted round these defences, and returned to bolster up morale by repeating these boasts and assuring the German people that a successful invasion was impossible. Although their defences were immensely strong, the German claim

that they could be equally strong along the whole coast line was ridiculous. These defences included natural caverns on the coast, which the Germans had made invulnerable to bombing attacks from the air (left); gigantic guns in immensely strong positions (right); massed anti-tank obstacles, road blocks, entrenchments, and minefields. Huge bomb-proof shelters of steel and concrete were erected to house U-boats. Many o. these fortified positions were built by the Todt organization, which used forced labour from the occupied countries.

BRITISH GUNS COVER THE FINAL ASSAULT ON THE ENEMY IN SICILY

NEXT MEDITERRANEAN PHASE
British troops at Catania ready for the invasion of the Italian mainland.

Made and printed in Great Britain by Odhams (Watford) Ltd., Watford. Copyright S.855.R.8.P.